Projective Coaching Techniques

Peter Freeth

GeniusMedia
CREATING KNOWLEDGE

2020

Projective Coaching Techniques

First Edition: February 2020 (1.1)

ISBN 978-1-908293-53-4

Genius Media 2020

Genius Media

B1502

PO Box 15113

Birmingham

B2 2NJ

geniusmedia.pub

books@geniusmedia.pub

For information about coaching and training programs, visit:

geniusnlp.com

genius.coach

For more projective coaching treasures to satiate desires both subtle and gross, visit:

projective.coach

For Emma, my inspiration

A Map of Sorts

We are the music makers, and we are the dreamers of dreams

Willy Wonka

No man has the right to dictate what other men should perceive, create or produce, but all should be encouraged to reveal themselves, their perceptions and emotions, and to build confidence in the creative spirit.

Ansel Adams

We all see only that which we are trained to see.

Robert Anton Wilson

Your visions will become clear only when you can look into your own heart. Who looks outside, dreams; who looks inside, awakes.

C.G. Jung

Until you make the unconscious conscious, it will direct your life and you will call it fate.

C.G. Jung

Introduction

You will need:
A piece of paper

Take a piece of paper. Hold it in front of you. What do you see?

"Nothing, it's blank!" you say. But is it *really* blank?

Look more carefully. What do you see?

Imperfections? Reflections? Shadows?

When you first looked at the paper, you saw what you expected to see – nothing. On closer inspection, you find that there is always something to see.

Now let's look *through* the paper.

What does this piece of paper represent?

What does it mean to you? What does it mean for you?

What do you notice about the edges?

Do the edges make the paper free or constrained?

Are the edges barriers to limit you or to keep you safe?

Have you considered the other side of the paper yet?

Have you considered the third dimension of the paper yet, its thickness?

As you can see, it's not just a piece of paper. It's a blank canvas, a space within which your imagination can play, a window through which we can glimpse your innermost unconscious fears, doubts, hopes and dreams.

This simple piece of paper is whatever you want it to be.

It represents limitless potential, an unanswered question, a road that leads over the horizon.

This piece of paper is a self portrait. By exploring what we can do with this, and other coaching tools, you will gain insights that you never imagined, and answer questions that you never thought it possible to ask.

The projective coaching tools that I will share with you in this book open up a whole new world of exploration with your clients. You can use them with one client or with groups. You can use them over and over again and get different results each time. You can use them to explore when questions are not helping and you can use them for the clients and the situations when words are simply not enough.

What if we took this piece of paper, this self portrait, and put it in a frame?

How does it look now?

Does the frame suit the contents?

What if we try a different frame?

Does the frame make a difference to how the contents appear? If so, why is that?

Now let's look at some colours.

Are there any that you like or dislike? Are there any missing?

What do these colours mean to you?

Some colours are given a generalised social significance – red for stop and green for go, for example. Or is it red for danger? Or red for excitement? Or red for hot? Or green for calm?

Red means stop when it's used within a certain frame, such as the frame of a traffic light. When it's in the frame of a psychometric profile, it might mean dominant, which might be good or bad… depending.

Aside from the meanings that other people attach to these colours, what do they mean to you?

How about these shapes? What meaning do they convey?

In this book, and with a projective approach to coaching, what we are working with is the subjective meaning that the client projects onto the world. In that regard, everything in the client's reality is a blank canvas onto which they project their hopes, fears, doubts and dreams. However, we are so attached to the idea of an objective reality that is 'out there' that it can often be difficult to get a client to accept the notion that they are creating reality for themselves. Their boss was mean to them, they were denied a fair opportunity, an unhappy relationship is someone else's fault, and they are so attached to their version of the facts that it can take some effort on your part to get them to see themselves as actors within that frame.

Of course, you're thinking that this is what a good coach does anyway – get the client to take responsibility, reframe meanings, change perspective and so on. Yes, yes. Very good, and well worth the years of training you've endured.

But it doesn't matter how good a coach you are, what matters is whether your client chooses to play along with your clever questions. Often, an evasive client will try to take control of the coaching conversation, and the ways in which they do this can be so subtle that the session is long finished before the coach realises what just happened. For example, the client might come with an agenda for the session, or might present an urgent problem at the start of the session. The former makes the coach think that the client is really taking their development seriously, the latter distracts the coach from what they were going to focus on. A good coach will add to the agenda, and use the presenting problem as an example through which to explore the deeper patterns. And whether you are a good coach, or an average coach, or a mediocre coach, you still need a way to do that, a way to shift the conversation onto your agenda, a way to sidestep the client's attempts to maintain their status quo, despite the obvious fact that they are paying you to help them change it. I won't go into the reasons why clients do that, because that's covered in my book Coaching Excellence. Suffice to say, the less the client is aware of the reasons for their avoidance behaviour, the harder it is to challenge cognitively, through coaching questions.

Projective techniques are widely used in psychotherapy, so I do wonder why these are not more widely adopted in coaching. These techniques are interesting, fun, and they can very quickly change the dynamic of a coaching relationship, taking you in new directions and opening up new conversations in an engaging, interactive and gentle way.

Projective techniques are often divided into five groups[1].

Associative techniques in which a particular stimulus is used to elicit the first thing that occurs in the client's mind. The set of symbols and colours that you recently saw in this book were examples of associative techniques, and the Rorschach test is perhaps the most well-known.

Completion techniques in which the client completes sentences or drawings, perhaps adding an ending or caption.

Constructive techniques in which the client creates a drawing, sculpture or story with minimal initial framing. The Mandala which you will read about later in this book is an example of a constructive techniques, although the initial setup script and the use of the circle do offer a frame of reference for the client.

Ordering techniques in which the client chooses from a group, or puts a group of pictures, statements or other fragments of information into a particular order.

Expressive techniques in which the client organises and incorporates a particular stimulus into a self-expressive process, such as role playing or an improvised story.

Relational techniques are a sixth group that I would add, in which the client organises a set of elements in a two or three dimensional space. This group would include the Three Circles and the Untangler which you'll read about later in this book, as well as constellation techniques as pioneered by Virginia Satir. I think that this is a distinct group from ordering, because such one dimensional techniques are about prioritising, which does not explain the complex interactions between elements in multiple dimensions.

---

1   Linzey, G. (1959). On the classification of projective techniques. Psychological Bulletin, 56(2), 158–168.

The Unsticker, which you will also read about later in this book, contains all of these techniques, presented randomly to the client.

Many psychologists, philosophers and self-help experts have said that language becomes a barrier to our experience of life, in that we may have limited scope for self expression through language, whereas there are many other forms of symbolic communication available to us, such as music, metaphor and imagery.

Alfred Korzybski, the creator of General Semantics, wrote in his book Science and Sanity, "Once we differentiate, differentiation becomes the denial of identity. Once we discriminate among the objective and verbal levels, we learn 'silence' on the unspeakable objective levels, and so introduce a most beneficial neurological 'delay' - engage the cortex to perform its natural function."

Korzybski wasn't known for speaking in layman's terms. What I think he's trying to say is that once we apply linguistic labels to our experience of life, we no longer experience life objectively, and the process of identification of what we see, hear and feel creates a window of opportunity within which we can change what we see, hear and feel. In this regard, General Semantics has some interesting connections with Cognitive Behavioural Therapy.

Linguistic determinism is the idea that language and its structures limit and determine human knowledge or thought, as well as thought processes such as categorisation, memory, and perception. The central idea is that people who speak different native languages have different internal thought processes.

Linguistic determinism is also related to linguistic relativity, known as the Sapir–Whorf hypothesis, which argues that we experience the world based on the structure of the language we use.

I think that the most important counter-argument is that we don't know what's going on in someone else's head, so if they lack a way to describe an experience, that doesn't mean that they didn't experience it. Consider the stereotype of the teenager whose emotional vocabulary exists only in the range of 'like' to 'don't like'. A person who is experiencing life in a way that they have never experienced it before will lack the means of expressing that to others, however, just because they lack a concise definition of their experience, that doesn't mean that they are not capable of experiencing it, or articulating it in a clumsy or roundabout way.

According to Guy Deutscher writing in the New York Times magazine in 2010, "Whorf announced, Native American languages impose on their speakers a picture of reality that is totally different from ours, so their speakers would simply not be able to understand some of our most basic concepts, like the flow of time or the distinction between objects (like "stone") and actions (like "fall"). For decades, Whorf's theory dazzled both academics and the general public alike. In his shadow, others made a whole range of imaginative claims about the supposed power of language, from the assertion that Native American languages instil in their speakers an intuitive understanding of Einstein's concept of time as a fourth dimension to the theory that the nature of the Jewish religion was determined by ancient Hebrew tenses.

Eventually, Whorf's theory crash-landed on hard facts and solid common sense, when it transpired that there had never actually been any evidence to support his fantastic claims.

The reaction was so severe that for decades, any attempts to explore the influence of the mother tongue on our thoughts were relegated to the loony fringes of disrepute. But 70 years on, it is surely time to put the trauma of Whorf behind us. And in the last few years, new research has revealed that when we learn our mother tongue, we do after all acquire certain habits of thought that shape our experience in significant and often surprising ways."

The article goes on to argue that languages which assign gender to everything force the speaker to reveal the gender of the people they're talking about. For example, in English I can talk about a colleague without saying that this person is male or female, but in German their gender would be revealed. I would present a counter-argument as follows. Firstly, if I told a German colleague that I was going to sit on a chair, that colleague would not think that I was sitting on a man, just because chair is a male word in German. Secondly, changing gender roles and distinctions in society will force changes in language. I don't think that there are no 'gender fluid' individuals in Germany, just because they don't have a suitable pronoun. Witness the fuss over the use of he/she/they that is going on in the media, and the creation of Mx as an alternative to Mr, Mrs, Miss or Ms, and the preceding creation of Ms for women who didn't want to reveal their marital status. What I think this shows us is that language may well influence how we think, but it does not constrain our experience of life, and we will readily create and modify language in order to define new experiences.

Every technology has its own associated language to describe things that the ordinary man-in-the-street doesn't need to talk about. As you read this book, you are not concerned with the font kerning. As you warm up your coffee in the microwave oven, you are are not thinking about the shape of the waveguide. As you check your messages on your smartphone, you are not wondering whether the display is TFT or OLED. You don't need to know about it, you don't need to talk about it and you don't have a word for it. Yet, even in your work, you use jargon which you wouldn't expect to hear in the street, and there is language that you use with your colleagues that you would translate when speaking to someone from outside of your set of working relationships.

As I mentioned, language is only one form of communication symbol. Through the projective techniques described in this book, you will have access to many more with which to explore the complex reality of your clients. You never know, you might gain some insights into your own reality too.

Every symbol is a generalisation of some original sensory data, and that sensory data is itself a diminished representation of what's going on in the outside world. Our eyes can only detect light waves within a very limited range, our ears can only respond to pressure variations in the air within a very limited range. Our temperature receptors only activate within a very limited range. The world only looks the way that it does because light, reflected off the surfaces around you, interacts with the cells in your retinas to produce electrochemical signals. Those light waves are actually radiating in every direction from every point on every surface. We simply can't see the light that's not heading directly into our eyes.

We humans are very good at pushing uncomfortable feelings away and distracting ourselves, and you might find that the techniques in this book bring those issues up to the surface where the client can no longer pretend that everything is OK.

Usually, everyone around them knows that 'things' are not OK anyway.

This reveals an interesting aspect of all of these projective techniques.

The Wikipedia entry for 'Projective test' lists the following assumptions made about projective techniques used in psychotherapy in a section entitled 'Concerns':

1. The more unstructured the stimuli, the more examinees reveal about their personality.

2. Projection is greater to stimulus material that is similar to the examinee

3. There is an "unconscious."

4. Subjects are unaware of what they disclose

5. Provides information about personality that is not obtainable through self-report measures.

6. Subjects are projecting their personality onto the ambiguous stimuli they are interpreting.

Aside from the obvious point that Wikipedia is user-edited, and that there is no reference for these concerns, I think it's worth exploring the assumptions listed.

On the first point, humans create meaning as a relationship between content and structure. Our language, for example, requires the right words (content) to be placed in the right order (structure), otherwise sense does make the communication not. As you can see, when the content is familiar and expected within a broader context, you can make allowances for missing structure. The more structure we give the client, the more we are dictating the meaning. For example, if I ask you how you feel then you have complete freedom to answer however you want, whereas if I ask you to rate how happy you feel on a scale of 1 to 5 then I limit your responses. You might not describe how you're feeling as happy in any way, but you have to fit your emotional experience to the limits I've imposed in order to answer.

Another way of looking at this is that the client will always project their personality onto the world, whether you think you have imposed structure or not. What I have found is that people come up with all kinds of subtle and creative ways to stamp their individuality on what they do and how they communicate, and if you have imposed a structure that they want to break, they will break it. For example, in the Mandala technique, the client is asked to draw a circle on a piece of paper. It's quite common for clients to draw the circle too big for the paper, so that only part of the circle is actually visible.

In order for communication to have meaning, there must be some kind of shared structure. Earlier, I showed you some shapes and asked you what they meant to you. Without a shared understanding of these symbols, we could not use them to communicate.

On the second point, I'm not sure how an ink blot or colour can be said to be 'similar to the examinee'. Even Stephen Covey said, "We see the world, not as it is, but as we are", in that our perceptual process is inseparable from the mind that creates it. You only need to take a look around your home or workspace to see how you have created an environment which is a map of your mind. My belief is that we project equally, regardless of the familiarity of the 'stimulus material', however that relevance may be more or less obvious to an external observer.

On the third point, it doesn't actually matter if there is an unconscious mind or not. If we define the unconscious in the way suggested by Freud or Jung, as a latent, dark place where innermost desires and fears lurk, then these projective techniques serve to raise those drivers into conscious awareness. If, on the other hand, we define 'unconscious' as 'anything which you're not currently thinking about' then again, these techniques are bringing those forgotten needs and drives to your attention. I'm sure you've had the experience of pushing a niggling worry to the back of your mind and distracting yourself with some important activity, only to later find that you weren't doing a very good job of distracting yourself because your friends or colleagues could easily see that you were worried. If this is the case then these techniques serve the valuable purpose of reminding you of the importance of thoughts which you believed you had dismissed but which are still lurking in the background.

On the fourth point, it's only relevant that the client knows or doesn't know what they're disclosing if you are making a judgement or diagnosis, which I strongly urge you to avoid. Whilst that may be true for the psychotherapeutic origins of some of these techniques, it is certainly not their relevance for us as coaches. If you've seen the film 'Watchmen' then there is a scene in a prison where a psychiatrist is evaluating one of the main characters, aptly named Rorschach. The viewer sees the true horrors inside the character's mind, whilst he answers the psychiatrist with "a pretty butterfly", "some nice flowers" and "clouds". Rorschach assumed that he knew what the 'right' answers would be, or he was just showing his disdain for the psychiatrist, but either way this point is based on the idea that the interpreter knows what he or she is looking for in response to the test. It's more likely that no-one really knows what an ink blot is 'supposed' to look like. Maybe it just looks like an ink blot.

On the fifth point, that projective tests provide information that is not available directly from the client, I would say that this is true for one of two reasons; either the client is unable to provide the information, or they are unwilling.

Why would the client be unable to tell you what's really going on for them? They might lack the awareness or vocabulary to article their experience. I don't mean that they might be stupid, I mean that they might be experiencing something that they have no frame of reference for, such as a client in career coaching who has been promoted to a senior position for the first time, or is facing redundancy for the first time, and can't easily explain how they feel about it.

The client might be unwilling for obvious reasons – they do not yet trust you with that information, perhaps for fear of how you will judge them. It's up to you to build that trust.

On the sixth and final point, that 'subjects are projecting their personality', we first have to figure out what 'personality' is. I put it to you that personality is not something that you have, it is a way that other people label their experience of you. When you are alone, I suspect you don't think about your personality, you only think about what's going on around you. Are you hungry? Thirsty? Do you like this TV program, or not like it? Reality is 'out there'. As a coach, you have probably got your head round the idea that reality is not out there, it is in here, inside your head, talking to you right now. Logically, you know that the sensory systems which relate information about the outside world are within your body, and therefore your experience of reality is inside your body, and therefore reality is inside your body. Still, it's a tricky idea to live with in practice, and no matter how 'good' a coach you are, there are times when you blame other people for your mood, or for the bad traffic, or for the events of your life. That Zen-like sense of self-awareness is hard to maintain when you're stubbing your toe on that stupid thing that some idiot left by the door.

Think of someone you work with. How would you describe their personality? Are you really describing their reaction to external events and to other people? If they are kind, or arrogant, or selfish, or patient, then those are relational definitions. A person cannot be arrogant alone. Even if you think that a person can be patient with a hobby, without anyone else being involved, then you are forgetting the most important person of all; you, the observer, watching this patient person and comparing their behaviour to your own. And so you might say, "Oh, I could never do that, I wouldn't have the patience." If we define personality as an observers assessment of your behaviour over time in relation to external stimuli then of course a person will project their personality, because they are responding to the stimuli as they would to any stimuli – based on the rules that they have learned over the course of their lifetime.

When you see an apple, what do you do with it? What if you see an old lady struggling to get across a busy road? What do you do when you see a friend's new baby for the first time? In all of these scenarios you know what to do, you follow the rules that you have learned, and you behave in a predictable way which an external observer would call your personality. And hence, it's quite possible for people to be wrong about your personality, when they only experience you in a narrow aspect of your life. You have probably had the experience of working with someone and thinking that you knew them, only to see a very different aspect of their personality at the Christmas party, or when they were feeling stressed. You might have said that they behaved "out of character" when in reality they behaved quite *in* character, to events or stimuli which you had never seen them interacting with before. Therefore, of course we project our personality, in that we deal with a stimulus according to rules, and those rules will be the source of our greatest weaknesses and also our greatest strengths. The only difference between the two is our level of awareness.

I can't stress enough that the point of using projective techniques is not to form some kind of objective, expert judgement about the client, but instead to provide novel points of reference for a valuable conversation.

When you use projective methods and techniques in your work, you do not know what anything 'means'. You maybe have read about symbology or numerology but you must remember that these are systems that were made up by someone and then generalised to apply to everyone. Gravity applies equally to everyone. The meaning of the number 3 does not. Different cultures have different interpretations so there is no universal meaning. Whatever an image or pattern looks like to you is irrelevant, what it looks like to your client is all that matters. Of course, you might offer your ideas, but you are not imposing them, you are not divining the answers. This is coaching, and your client is not paying you enough for you to do all the work.

These techniques are shared to help you to have richer, diverse, interesting, valuable conversations with your clients. As conversation starters, I find them invaluable.

The use of projective tests in psychotherapy is a matter of debate, however psychotherapists do seem to be fond of labelling conditions, and the Diagnostic and Statistical Manual volume 5 lists 157 psychiatric 'disorders'. New additions in the latest volume include "intermittent explosive disorder" and "compulsive hoarding". It is important to note two points about the DSM; firstly, it classifies conditions based on symptoms, and secondly, it is used by medical insurance companies when deciding whether to pay out.

As a coach, you might well see such 'disorders' as being outside of the remit of your work, and I would agree. I also feel that categorising symptoms in this way can lead to the reduction of an individual to a condition. I also personally feel that many of the 'disorders' listed are in fact normal operation of the human machine, attempting to rebalance itself in the face of conflicting information or pressures.

I do find it interesting that many coaches would reject the diagnoses of the psychiatrist, yet would happily use profiling tools to diagnose a client's personality. I won't get into a debate here on the subject of such tools, but suffice to say I do not use them.

A human being is a complex system, and some experts are keen to point out that there is no 'normal'. Remember that in 1952, the pioneer of modern computing Alan Turning was convicted of "gross indecency", a criminal offence in the UK at the time, based on a law passed in 1885. In the late 19th century, women suffering from post-natal depression would be consigned to a lunatic asylum and separated from their families. Clearly, our understanding of the complex software of humanity has developed dramatically, and perhaps we still have a long way to go before we can genuinely welcome all possible states of mind into the realm of 'normality'.

Your role as a coach, as I am sure you are well aware, is not to judge or diagnose but to enrich and support, to provide space for your clients to grow beyond their experiences, and through the shared exploration, to enable your own growth.

The bottom line for you is this: If, as a coach, you restrict yourself to cognitively questioning your clients then you are missing a significant opportunity to interact in a way which transcends words, and you are denying your clients the opportunity to express themselves, free from the vocabulary which they are able or willing to use. By exploring these, and other projective techniques, you open up a whole new avenue of exploration and expression, and free yourself and your clients to truly explore the world of their dreams.

Three Circles

You will need:
A blank sheet of paper or a notebook
A pen or pencil

Take your sheet of paper and drawing implement. I want you to draw three circles, anywhere on the piece of paper, as large or small as you like.

The three circles represent:

1. You

2. Your team or contemporaries

3. Your employer or clients

Do that now. I'll wait.

OK, let's now explore what you have drawn and why.

These circles do not 'mean' anything in themselves. You are not a soothsayer, making a divination, and you are certainly not a psychotherapist, staring over your half-rimmed glasses and tutting disapprovingly at your client's obvious character flaws.

The value in this exercise is in the questions that you ask, and hence it is an excellent starting point from which to explore projective coaching.

The client will draw whatever they draw, and if you're doing this as a solitary exercise, then the client will largely be unaware of how else they could have drawn the circles. This exercise works very well in a group context too, as people can then compare their drawings with each other.

If you consider all of the possible ways that the three circles could have been drawn then you can ask your client to interpret what they have unconsciously created.

There are a number of ways in which these diagrams can differ, so let's explore each in turn.

Size

Do the circles fill the paper?

Relative size

Are the circles the same size as each other?

Spacing

What space is there between the circles?

Are they equally spaced from each other?

Are they being pulled together or pushed apart?

Hierarchy

Is any hierarchy implied through size or position?

Overlap

Do the circles touch or overlap?

Are any circles inside others?

Neatness

Are the circles circular?

Are the circles more, or less than a circle?

Labels

Did the client label the circles? Why?

If there are labels, are they inside or outside the circles? Why?

You're probably wondering if the three circles always have to represent the subject, their team and their employer. In fact, the circles can represent anything you like, such as:

- Past, Present, Future
- Me, You, Relationship
- Us, Customers, Competitors

You can see that the identities of the three circles define the relationships between them. Where the client may not be able or willing to define those relationships cognitively, especially if they are in a work scenario, they will express their feelings symbolically and you can then ask questions to interact with those feelings and relationships.

Let's look at some different examples of how the three circles might be drawn. This isn't an exhaustive list, but it will give you some ideas for what to look for and ask about when you first use this exercise with your clients.

You can see some differences in spacing, hierarchy and relative size here.

What seems to be expressed through the way the three circles are drawn is a sense of the subject's relationship within a bigger system. For example, does the subject feel part of a team, or do they feel like an outsider? Regardless of what their job title or organisation chart suggests, they might feel disconnected from their colleagues. The size of the circles also seems to suggest how important or relevant a person feels within a team. This can, of course, result from a number of factors, and can reveal information about how individuals are recognised, or the type of work that they are doing, or something that is not directly connected with the workplace at all.

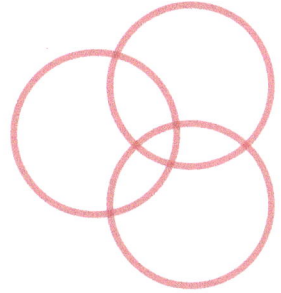
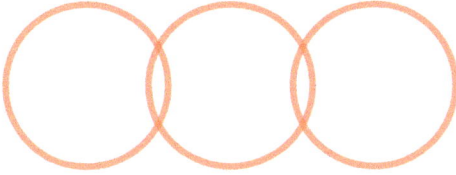

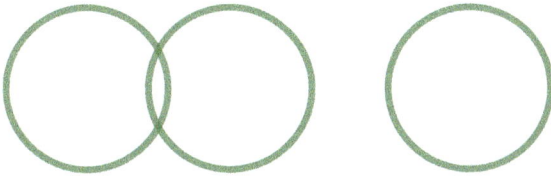

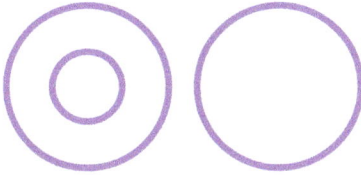

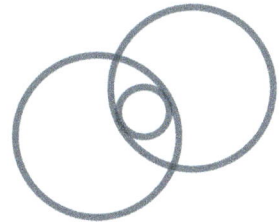

I expect you'd like to see some real examples, so here are 8 diagrams drawn by the members of a corporate team during a conflict resolution workshop.

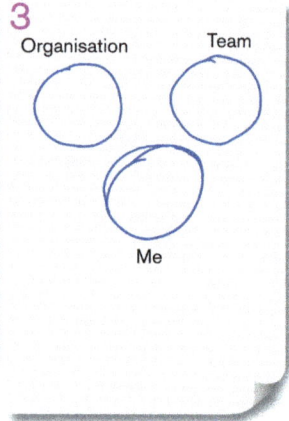

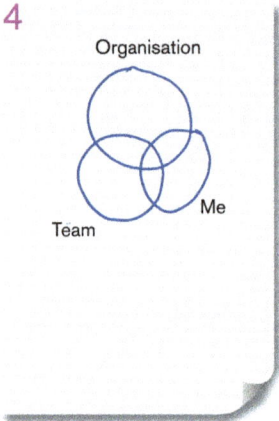

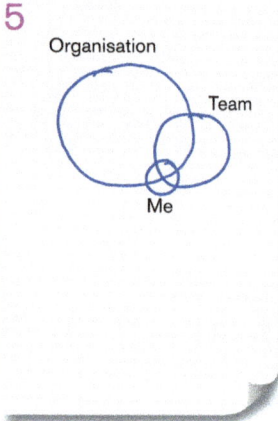

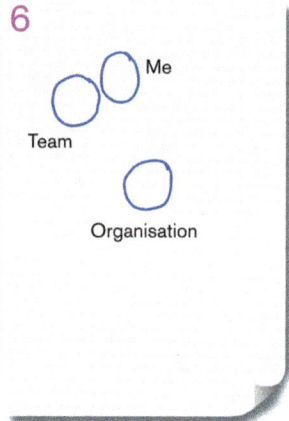

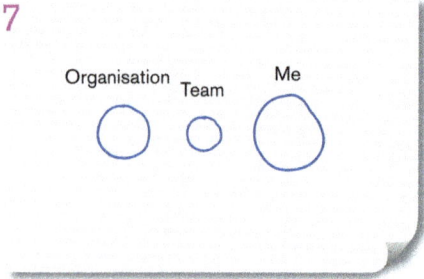

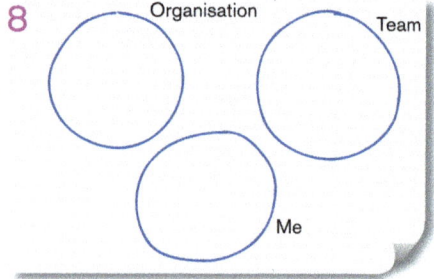

Notice the circle sizes, both relative to each other, and relative to the paper. What clues do these diagrams give you about how the individuals might feel about themselves, the organisation and each other? How might this influence your approach?

If you're hoping that I will tell you what these diagrams mean then I have to disappoint you. I don't know what they mean. I can guess, based both on the drawings and of my knowledge of the people involved, but the important point again is that you get your clients to explore what the diagrams mean for them.

An exercise like this has tremendous value in both a group and an individual scenario. In both cases, there seem to be two very important points about the use of this exercise that are worth noting.

Firstly, the subject draws the circles without first knowing how they will be interpreted, so they express far more honesty than if they were openly asked to talk about their relationship to a team and organisation. This is especially true when a team is working together in a group activity.

Secondly, once the team have explored and compared drawings and reach conclusions about their meanings, the drawings cannot be undone.

As a coach facilitating this exercise, you must therefore be extremely tactful. With some experience, you'll begin to see correlations between the drawings and the behaviour of the individuals in the team. Just because this information is available doesn't mean it has to be revealed. To do so too early can disengage people from the conversation, which is of course completely counter-productive.

You might find that members of a group are unwilling to voice interpretations that they think will be unpopular or unacceptable. For example, if a member of a team feels isolated or pushed out, and they draw their 'Me' circle far away from the 'Team' circle then they may not feel that they can say this in front of their colleagues, which is of course the reason that they might feel isolated anyway. In such a situation, you might not have the members of the team look at each others' drawings, instead giving them some ideas of how to interpret what they have drawn and then allowing them to explore that in private, or in a separate discussion with you.

Perhaps, after having the opportunity to explore privately, the members of the team might then be more willing to share aspects of their working experience which they had not done previously. In this way, the exercise serves to bring issues to the surface which otherwise go unexplored. Clearly, you need to use considerable tact and empathy in such a case.

Mandala

You will need:

Large plain paper or a sketchbook, preferably A3

A smaller sheet of paper or notebook, or download and print the template from mybook.li/pcmt

A pen or pencil to make notes with

A set of coloured pens or pencils - at least 12 different colours

mybook.li/pcmandala

Introduction

Mandala means 'circle' in Sanskrit. You have probably seen off-the-shelf mandalas featuring colourful geometric designs; this is quite different.

The Mandala is a window into your unconscious mind. It reveals elements, perspectives and relationships which you will not be consciously aware of, and yet when you see them in front of you, they will immediately make sense. It will be as if your unconscious mind, your psyche, even your soul is trying to tell you something. When you discover the messages contained within the Mandala, you will immediately recognise that message, like a whispered voice that you have been ignoring.

The result of the mandala can be extremely revealing, and I highly recommend this as a coaching exercise to use at the outset of a new coaching relationship, as it opens up the conversation to its broadest and most powerful level.

According to Wikipedia, "(The Mandala) originally meant to represent wholeness and a model for the organizational structure of life itself—a cosmic diagram that shows us our relation to the infinite, the world that extends beyond and within our minds and bodies." ... "According to art therapist and mental health counselor Susanne F. Fincher, we owe the re-introduction of mandalas into modern Western thought to Carl Jung, the Swiss analytical psychologist. In his pioneering exploration of the unconscious through his own art making, Jung observed the motif of the circle spontaneously appearing. The circle drawings reflected his inner state at that moment. Familiarity with the philosophical writings of India prompted Jung to adopt the word "mandala" to describe these circle drawings he and his patients made. In his autobiography, Jung wrote:

I sketched every morning in a notebook a small circular drawing, which seemed to correspond to my inner situation at the time. Only gradually did I discover what the mandala really is: the Self, the wholeness of the personality, which if all goes well is harmonious. (Carl Jung, Memories, Dreams, Reflections, p195).

Jung recognized that the urge to make mandalas emerges during moments of intense personal growth. Their appearance indicates a profound re-balancing process is underway in the psyche. The result of the process is a more complex and better integrated personality.

The mandala serves a conservative purpose - namely, to restore a previously existing order. But it also serves the creative purpose of giving expression and form to something that does not yet exist, something new and unique. The process is that of the ascending spiral, which grows upward while simultaneously returning again and again to the same point. (Jungian analyst Marie-Louise von Franz, C. G. Jung: Man and His Symbols, p. 225)

According to the psychologist David Fontana, its symbolic nature can help one "to access progressively deeper levels of the unconscious, ultimately assisting the meditator to experience a mystical sense of oneness with the ultimate unity from which the cosmos in all its manifold forms arises."''

Personally, I simply find the Mandala to be a fun and creative way to explore complex issues which are just outside of the client's conscious awareness.

Creating the Mandala

Take a blank sheet of paper and your set of coloured pens or pencils.

Place the paper in front of you and your pens or pencils to the side.

Sit comfortably and relax.

Close your eyes for a moment and allow your mind to drift. If you find yourself distracted by stray thoughts or reminders of things you don't want to forget, take a pen and notepad and make a list. Capture each important distracting thought, because it is important, and as you write each down, allow yourself to hit the mental snooze button, safe in the knowledge that you will still remember all the important things you need to remember, and that right now, as you take a moment to write now anything that comes to mind, you can focus right now on the next part of this important exercise.

As you allow your mind to drift, as you allow yourself to relax, you might begin to notice scenes, shapes, colours, movement, images, dark, light. Merging, drifting, wondering.

In a moment, you will open your eyes and choose the first colour which speaks to you, the first colour which draws your attention. Be guided by your intuition.

Open your eyes and choose a colour.

Draw a circle on the paper in front of you, as large as possible.

And now, continue to draw whatever shapes and colours you feel drawn to within the circle. Draw as much as you like for as long as you like. Continue to draw and express the shapes and colours and images that you imagined. Allow your colours and hand to be guided by your unconscious mind. Without pausing to judge or question or wonder, allow your pen or pencil to wander freely over the paper, making whatever marks you feel, drawing whatever shapes and forms you feel, in the colours you feel.

When you feel that your drawing is complete, you can pause.

This drawing in a circle is called a Mandala. It contains the beginnings of your map.

Creating a Key

Every map has a list of symbols, known as a 'key' or 'legend'. There isn't space on the map to write every feature that you might be interested in, so the key is a way to simplify the map without losing the important information. Here's an example:

Symbol	Description	Symbol	Description
	Art gallery (notable / important)		Museum
	Boat hire		National Trust
	Boat trips		Nature reserve
	Building of historic interest		Other tourist feature
	Cadw		Parking
	Camp site	P&R	Park and ride, all year
	Camping and caravan site	P&R	Park and ride, seasonal
	Caravan site		Phone; public, emergency
	Castle or fort		Picnic site

Although you may not realise it yet, your mandala is a map, and it has a key of its own, and that key will unlock the secrets that your unconscious mind has placed in your map for you to find.

In this step, you will create the key for your map, which will include three elements: colours, numbers and shapes. We collectively call these elements 'symbols'. If you look at the map key above, you will see the colours blue, red and black, some shapes such as star, triangle, square, and some numbers such as 5 (the points on the star) and 2 (telephones).

We're going to work through your mandala to decode the key, and I'll show you some real examples from other mandalas to help you.

Interpreting your Mandala

Colours

Begin by looking at your mandala. You will see shapes and colours. The colours are easy to recognise and list out - green, red, pink, blue etc. You can download a template to use from mybook.li/pcmt or you can simply make a list in a notebook. At this stage, do not try to make sense of any colours, shapes or numbers, simply list them out.

In this example, you can see the colours yellow, pink, purple, grey, turquoise and blue.

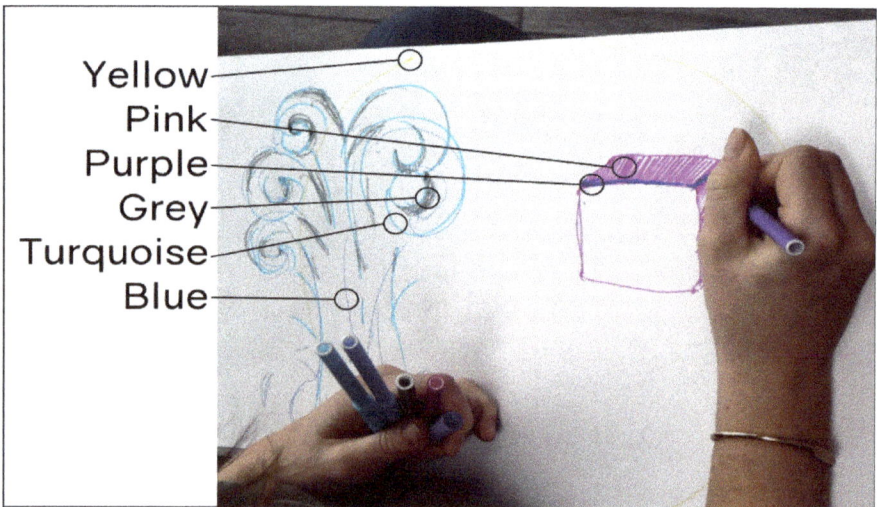

Do remember to list white as a colour. Your mandala contains white space, and it's there for a reason.

Numbers

You might look at your mandala and think that there are no numbers, however there are many. In the mandala, numbers mean the number of times that a particular shape appears. For example, if you draw three triangles then you have the number 3. If you draw a square, then you have the numbers

1 and 4 - 1 for the number of squares, and 4 for the lines forming the square.

In this next example, you can see the colours brown, blue, pink and yellow. You can also see some simple shapes; circles, stars, triangles.

The shapes might be more difficult to identify at first, because you aren't looking at what you've drawn, you're looking at what you think you've drawn. Here's an example.

If you had drawn this, you might see a sun and a flower, because those are the objects that you were thinking about. In fact, your unconscious mind is expressing ideas and dreams through your drawing, and those ideas and dreams are abstract. As you draw, you try to make sense of those abstract ideas, and you draw shapes as a result.

Think of all the different ways that you could draw a flower:

As you can see, it's not just a simple matter of drawing a flower. The type of flower is significant, because each is made up of different component shapes, and those shapes tell a story because they were not chosen randomly.

At this stage, do not try to make sense of any colours, shapes or numbers, simply list them out.

Shapes

If we take a step back, we can see that in this mandala image there are 3 colours, red, green and yellow, and there are 6 circles - two large and four small. Do you see them? You can also see some lines. The yellow circle has 10 straight lines radiating from it. Now look at the red circle. Its lines are curved - except for one. If we only see that shape as a flower then we see the lines as petals. In fact, they are lines - so for the red shape we might list out:

Petals: 10

Stems: 1

Curved lines: 10

Straight lines: 1

So now we have a yellow circle with 10 straight lines, and a red circle with 10 curved lines and 10 petals. Do you think that's a coincidence? Of course not!

Similarly, we have 4 green circles, and 4 sides to the yellow square, and 4 triangles around the edges of the yellow square.

Look at the shapes in this example:

What do you see: People? A river? A boat? Make sure you also notice the circles, triangles and lines. For example, there are 5 black circles, 4 purple circles, 5 small yellow circles, 1 large yellow circle and so on.

At this stage, do not try to make sense of any colours, shapes or numbers, simply list them out.

Here's an example of a mandala with a completed key:

When people draw mandalas, they will be absolutely certain that they didn't think about what they were drawing, and they didn't plan to draw objects that were connected through shapes, colours, and numbers, yet that's exactly what happens. Your unconscious mind is expressing your ideas and dreams in multiple ways, and the same messages will come through, over and over again.

This is the reason that we take a break between drawing your mandala and creating the key, so that you can more easily see the abstract symbols that you have drawn.

At the end of this step you will have a list of all the colours, numbers and shapes used in your mandala. If you're using the template, it might look something like this:

Colours		Numbers	
Colour	Meaning	Number	Meaning
Blue		1	
Green		2	
Yellow		3	
Red		4	
Black		6	
White		10	

Shapes		Combinations	
Shape	Meaning	Combination	Interpretation
Square			
Line			
Triangle			
Cloud			
Star			
V			
Cat			
House			

Believe it or not, you will very likely have missed some - that's OK, you can add them to your key later.

You will now have a list of all the symbols in your map, and if you're using the template (mybook.li/pcmt), you'll see that there is a space next to each symbol for you to write its meaning. Just a like a key for a road map, each symbol - a colour, shape or number - has a unique meaning.

It is important to understand that there is no universal interpretation for all mandalas, yours is unique. Even if you believe in numerology, numbers have no commonly held meaning, they only have a meaning that is unique for you. Ignore what anyone else says about the meanings of colours. Forget what you have been told, trust your intuition.

Choose the first item on your list; let's say it's the colour blue. Put your mandala out of your mind and think only about the colour blue. Don't think about a blue object, just imagine yourself surrounded by the colour. And when you think about that colour now, what does it mean to you?

Some people struggle to assign meanings to symbols at this stage. When asked what the colour blue means, for example, they might say that it's the sky. That's not a meaning. You must let go of your tendency to think literally and embrace the metaphorical language of your unconscious mind. As you imagine the colour blue now, what does it mean to you? What does it mean for you? What does it remind you of? How does it make you feel? You might think something like peace, calm, happiness, hope, freedom or whatever comes to mind for you. Remember, your key for your mandala is unique. You might make another mandala next month, and the meanings that you assign to your symbols might change. Your key is for this mandala, in this moment.

Work through your entire list of symbols, assigning meanings to each one. If you have a triangle, you might interpret it as security, or stability, or confusion, or choice, or anything else. Ask yourself, when you think about that shape, what does it mean to you? What does it mean for you?

Don't rush this stage, take as long as you need to create a key that you feel happy with. If you struggle to assign a meaning to a symbol, leave it and come back to it later. It's much better to complete this stage of the process with fresh eyes, where you're less likely to be restricted by literal interpretations.

At the end of this stage, your key will look something like this:

Colours		Numbers	
Colour	Meaning	Number	Meaning
Blue	Peace	1	Self
Green	Curiosity	2	Balance
Yellow	Happiness	3	Stability
Red	Energy	4	Trapped
Black	Unknown	6	Work
White	Possibility	10	End

Shapes		Combinations	
Shape	Meaning	Combination	Interpretation
Square	Trapped		
Line	Future		
Triangle	Confusion		
Cloud	Possibility		
Star	Faith		
V	Direction		
Cat	Escape		
House	Family		

Mandala Symbol Key   v1   © Genius Ltd 2020 genius.coach   ⭐Genius

Once you've completed your mandala's key, you can begin to interpret the messages that it contains for you.

Remember that every pen or pencil mark on your sheet of paper was put there by you, by choice. You have drawn nothing by accident or 'just because it looked nice'. There is a choice behind every mark - the same choice that drives you in your day to day life. By understanding the meaning hidden within the marks you have made, we can begin to understand and interpret the map for your life.

Combining

The first part of interpreting the mandala is combining the individual symbols to understand the meaning of the more complex objects within the mandala.

If you are using the template (mybook.li/pcmt) then you'll see an area for recording the combinations on your mandala.

In this part of your key, you will combine the elements of your map - the colours, numbers and shapes - to understand what they represent.

In this example, we have five turquoise swirls in the shape that looks like a water fountain. Let's imagine that the key for these three symbols looks like this:

5 = Freedom

Swirl = Time

Turquoise = Adventure

To combine these symbols, we simply merge them together into one, like this:

"When you think about Freedom, Time and Adventure, all together, what does all of this mean for you?"

In your mind, you now imagine combining Freedom, Time and Adventure all into one meaning, a single entity. What does this mean for you?

Try that now, with this example.

"When you think about Freedom, Time and Adventure, all together, what does all of this mean for you?"

Let's imagine that you said "Exploring". Now we know that the thing that looks like a fountain contains the meaning of 'exploring'. It contains other messages too, for example in the grey parts. We can find out what those other messages are and combine those.

Now let's look at the other part of the mandala above, the pink object. Remember that it's not a box, because a box is a three dimensional construct. If you see a pink box then you are projecting information which is not there in the mandala itself, and that will distort the meaning.

We might combine the following:

4 = Trapped

Pink = Woman

Line = Barrier

When you think of Trapped, Woman and Barrier, what does all of that mean for you? Let's say for the example that this means 'relationship'. You might say that a connection between trapped and relationship is bad, and it can't possibly mean that. Actually, for the person who drew the mandala above, that's exactly what it meant. You cannot project your own meaning into another person's mandala, we can only use it as an example to learn from.

Now we have two sides to the mandala above; on the left, exploring and on the right, relationship.

If you're using the template, it will now look something like this:

Colours		Numbers	
Colour	Meaning	Number	Meaning
Blue	Peace	1	Self
Green	Curiosity	2	Balance
Yellow	Happiness	3	Stability
Red	Energy	4	Trapped
Black	Unknown	6	Work
White	Possibility	10	End

Shapes		Combinations	
Shape	Meaning	Combination	Interpretation
Square	Trapped	Blue+2+Cloud	Dreams, Hopes
Line	Future	Red+6+Square	Frustration, Career
Triangle	Confusion	Black+1+Cat	Self-doubt
Cloud	Possibility	Yellow+1+Cat	Freedom
Star	Faith	Green+3+Line	Future plans
V	Direction		
Cat	Escape		
House	Family		

Mandala Symbol Key   v1   © Genius Ltd 2020 genius.coach   ⭐Genius

Connecting

The mandala reveals meaning within the objects you have drawn, and there is another layer of meaning concealed in the relationships and connections between those objects.

When you look at the arrangement of objects within your mandala, what do you notice?

What about their relative sizes?

What about the space between them? What is in that space? What does this mean for you?

Look at the example above again. What about the grey and blue parts? How do they connect?

Remember that every pen or pencil mark on your sheet of paper was put there by you, by choice. You have drawn nothing by accident or 'just because it looked nice'. There is a choice behind every mark - the same choice that drives you in your day to day life. By understanding the meaning hidden within the marks you have made, we can begin to understand and interpret the map for your life.

The Circle

Look at the circle in your mandala, the part you drew first.

The way that you have drawn the circle itself is important too. It's very unlikely that you have actually drawn a circle

In the example mandala above, the circle is yellow, but notice how it is not actually a circle - at the top, the circle runs off the page. And the fountain-like symbol on the left overlaps the circle. The instructions were the same ones that you followed - draw a circle, and then to draw within the circle. How is it significant that 'relationship' is inside the circle, and 'exploring' is partly outside?

Two of the turquoise swirls are inside the circle, three are outside. What might these represent?

Look at your own mandala again. Look at the first circle that you drew. Did you put exactly the right amount of effort in, or too little, or too much? What does this mean for you?

Too much   Not enough

Look at the shape of your circle. How circular is it? What does this mean for you?

Look at how much space is left on the paper outside of the circle. What does this mean for you?

Have you drawn any objects on or outside of the circle, rather than within it? What does this mean for you?

The circle is the only part of the mandala which does have a consistent meaning. The circle is **you**.

Remember that every pen or pencil mark on your sheet of paper was put there by you, by choice. You have drawn nothing by accident or 'just because it looked nice'. There is a choice behind every mark - the same choice that drives you in your day to day life. By understanding the meaning hidden within the marks you have made, we can begin to understand and interpret the map for your life.

Now that you have completed your interpretations for your mandala, you can move onto the final phase - using it as a map to explore the future.

Exploring

Hold your mandala in front of you at arm's length.

Rotate your mandala slowly so that you can see it from every angle, not only how you originally drew it.

Does it feel 'right' as you drew it? Or is there an orientation which seems more comfortable?

What might this mean?

Now, as you continue to hold your mandala in front of you, imagine that it is a window, a portal, and through this portal you can glimpse a world beyond the paper.

Imagine that you can walk up to the paper and through the circle into the world of your mandala.

Explore inside. Visit the various elements that you have drawn. Interact with them.

Notice any movement in your mandala.

Notice the spaces between the elements.

Notice any sounds that you might hear.

Explore the world of your mandala for as long as you like and then return back to 'this' world.

Extending

Look at your mandala again. What now seems to be missing from it?

Take your coloured pens or pencils again and add anything that you feel is missing or change anything that you now feel is not quite right.

Revisit your mandala's key and add any new elements and symbols.

Revisit the Decoding and Interpreting steps to understand the meaning of the changes you have made.

What does all of this mean for you?

Conclusion

As you look at the hidden messages that come out of your mandala, what do you see?

What meanings do you discover from this?

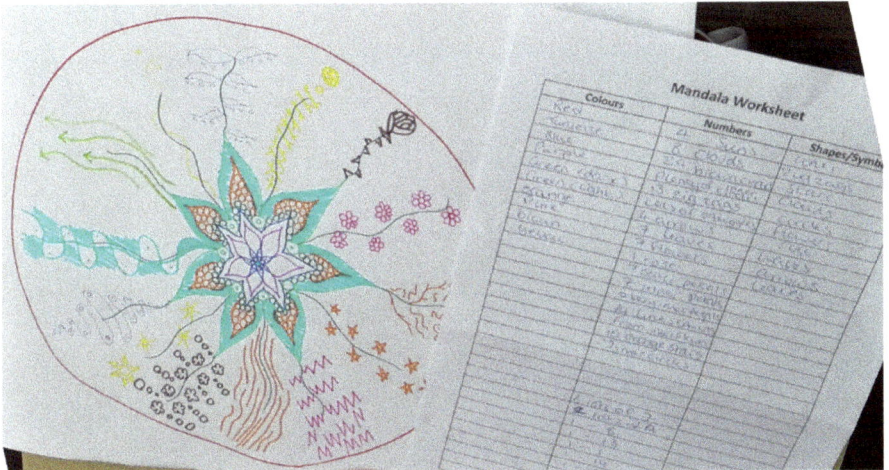

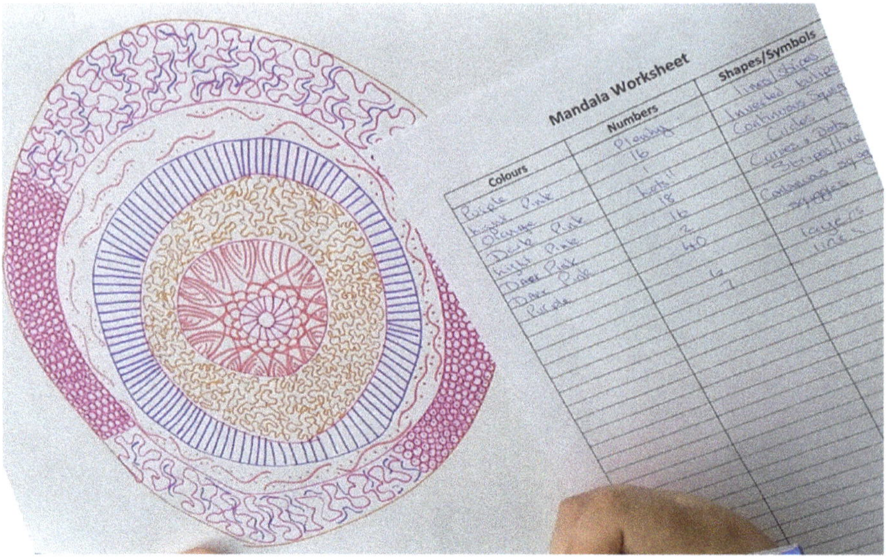
Mandala Worksheet
Colours
Numbers
Shapes/Symbols

Mandala Worksheet
Colours
Numbers
Shapes/Symbols

Pictures

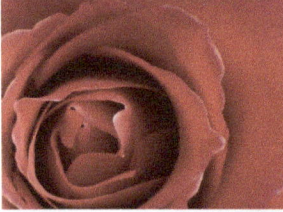

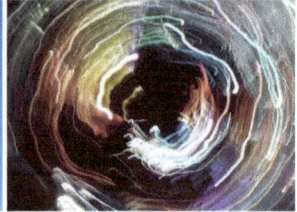

What do you make of these images?

Which ones appeal to you the most? Why do you think that is?

Which ones do you feel that you connect with most?

What do you think is happening as you look at the pictures?

Don't just skip over them, take time to study each one. Take time to notice the details that you might otherwise miss.

You can probably see that looking at images like this and creating meaning from them is an associative technique. The image is already created, and the meaning that you make of it reveals something about your psyche. Psychiatrists would use word and image association tests to deduce something about your mental state. The problem is, of course, that no-one knows what a 'normal' mental state is, and no-one knows what a 'correct' association is supposed to be. If you look at an ink blot and say that it looks like the devil, is that a bad thing? Or good

Associative techniques like this reveal something about your client's thought processes and state of mind, and there is no right or wrong answer, each image only serves as a starting point to provoke a new conversation.

Images can also be used as completion techniques, for example, looking at the image of the giraffe, what happens next, and what does that mean to you?

Images like this can also be used as expressive techniques, for example, to tell a story about the tree. You could also combine pictures, for example pick three pictures from the previous page and tell a story which links them together, and then consider how that story says something about your own life or current situation.

Rather than using images as a divinatory tool, you might use them as a conversation starter. I also find them useful as a group coaching tool. For example, in a culture change scenario, you might give participants a selection of images and invite them to group the images into categories, which you have either defined for them, or which they define themselves. You can even start by grouping and allow the categories to emerge later. In this case, the use of images would be an ordering or relational technique.

You might have figured out that there are many ways in which you can use such images, and therefore they are an excellent part of any coach's toolkit. I used to have a pack of photos which I had printed at a local supermarket's photo lab. The cost is very low, they're easy to carry around and you can use them in all kinds of situations as an indirect approach to the coaching conversation.

Another interesting projective aspect of pictures and photographs is in the messages that we knowingly and unknowingly send through social media. If you consider the photos that you post to Instagram, Facebook or similar, they all tell a story about you. You mostly post the same kinds of photos, about the same kinds of subjects, in order to tell a consistent story about how you want to be perceived by others.

These images are, of course, edited and censored, like any story that you tell about yourself. You portray your life as you want others to see it, and I suspect that you don't show your dirty dishes or the corner of the bedroom that never sees a duster. Equally, you don't show anything which contradicts your chosen story. If, for example, you want to show how you are independent and self-reliant, your photos will tend to show you alone rather than with your friends.

What messages do you see people communicating in this way? They might include:

- I am popular
- I have a busy social life
- I am important
- I am wanted
- I see the world in an unusual way
- I overcome many challenges
- I have an interesting life
- I need help
- I am lonely
- I am loved
- I am suffering
- I am healed
- I am an expert
- I am intelligent
- I am successful
- I am unlucky
- I am lucky
- I am an outsider
- I am free

Now take a look at the photos that you post to social media. What story are you telling?

As a general principle, if I am trying to prove something about myself, it's because I think that you think it's not true, or more simply, it's because I know it's not true. Take the example of certain populist politicians who go out of their way to tell us that everyone else is lying, and they are the only people who we can trust. They embellish answers to questions with unnecessary phrases – or at least phrases which are not necessary for someone who is being truthful, because if you're telling the truth, you don't need to first tell people that you're about to tell them the truth. Such phrases include:

- "To be honest"
- "To be absolutely honest"
- "To tell you the truth"
- "Believe me when I say"
- "Let me be clear"
- "The fact is"
- "As you already know"
- "And you can count on me when I say"

As I have already told you, and let me be very clear about this, the truth is that there is no need to signal your honesty if you are telling the truth. There is no need to provide a running commentary of your intentions, because your honest intentions are already assumed within the context of the conversation. We assume honesty because we expect it.

I'm not for a moment suggesting that your clients are liars, although there is a chapter by that title in my book Coaching Excellence. Your clients do not tell you the entire truth, they tell you a censored version of the truth. In short, when you are wholly reliant on language to interact with your clients, they will tell you an edited version of their story in order to create an intended response in you. For example, they might be trying to protect themselves from your judgement or criticism, and as much as you can say that you are not going to judge them, they know that you are, and you know that you are, because you have to judge them in order to make sense of their story. You might not judge them as being stupid or malicious, but you still reach a judgement.

Drawing

An obvious example of pictures as a projective technique is the use of free-form drawing. Without any explicit directions about what or how to draw, you can pose a 'framing question' and allow your client to express themselves through paper and coloured pens or pencils. This works well as both an individual and group exercise, and you can either interpret the symbols as you did with the Mandala, or you can use the drawings in a more literal sense, working with what the client thinks they have drawn in order for them to tell their story. By getting the client, or the clients in their team, to explore each others' stories, the hidden relationships and elements can be revealed in a gentle, non-directive way.

This is a significant difference from the approach you took with the Mandala, because in the Mandala you were looking for, and expecting the presence of, hidden information. In this free drawing techniques, you are not expecting any hidden information to be revealed, and you are not questioning your client on that basis. You are simply using the artistic process as an intermediary.

I find this to be very useful in group coaching. If you jump straight into talking about problems and solutions, it is very easy for individuals to take up defensive positions. The first, most important stage of any group process has to involve open, non-judgemental sharing and listening. Having clients draw their current position is a good way to do this, as it first gives them a non-verbal way to express themselves, and this serves to help them to articulate some of the more complex or controversial ideas that they hold.

Here are some examples of drawings produced by leaders in a strategy workshop in response to the frame of "Where am I now?". You can see how each person has interpreted and represented this differently; some symbolically, some literally, and all have presented an interesting and diverse set of personal emotions, experiences and intentions.

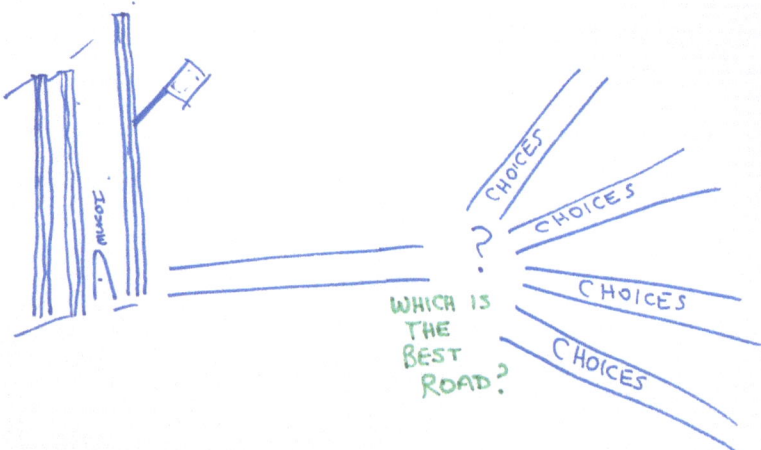

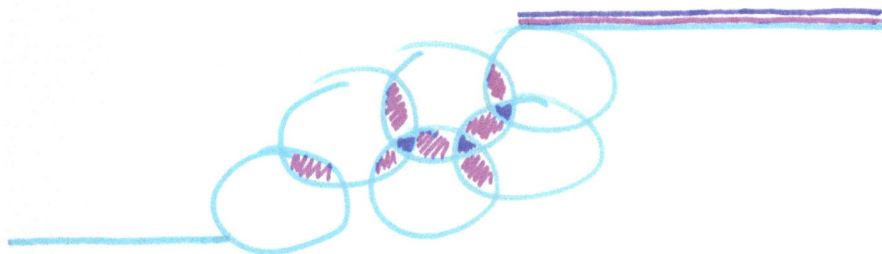

Revealing the Truth

Projective coaching techniques are not reliant on language, and through indirect means, can reveal hidden truths. For example, in a corporate coaching context, a client might not feel comfortable to talk candidly about their relationship with their manager. The three circles exercise would reveal this, and you would then carry the responsibility to conduct a tactful, sensitive and absolutely confidential conversation with that client. Having revealed the truth, the client is presented with only three realistic options:

1. Continue coaching and deny the truth

2. Stop coaching and explain this to their manager

3. Accept the truth and trust you

This might look like it puts the client into a corner, however it is a win-win situation. If the client who you have been contracted to work with cannot share the real background with you then your coaching will be frustrating for you and ineffective for the client. From your own ethical perspective, you want the coaching process to work, and if the client is preventing the process from working then you are better served by not engaging with that client.

If the client chooses option 1 then they are choosing to stay in the conversation with you, giving you an opportunity to earn their trust. It might take several sessions for them to fully accept the truth but the end result will be worth it. In a corporate talent management program, one client took 7 sessions before he stopped 'jamming' and told me something true. Jamming is the word I use to describe the noise that a client makes in order to prevent you from coaching them. It comes from the military meaning, in which an enemy will broadcast a radio signal on the same frequency as your signal in order to prevent you from communicating. The client in question once spent 45 minutes showing me the company's reward system which gave managers points to award to staff which could then be collected and swapped for gifts. More commonly, he would take up the entire coaching session telling me what a great job he was doing. I would end each session by telling him that we were both wasting our time and the best thing for him would be to stop coaching. I think that two factors kept him in the conversation; firstly, his need to show his managers that he was 'with the program', and secondly, his desire to address some personal issues that he thought he was doing a good job of hiding from everyone.

If the client chooses option 3 then they have realised, as Bugs Bunny would say, that 'the jig is up'. They trust you enough to at least enter into the conversation with you.

The most dangerous option for you is option 2. There is a real risk that the client will smile nicely at you throughout the coaching session, and then go away and tell their manager or the HR manager that they don't want to continue with the coaching because you are a very bad coach, or you were aggressive, or controlling, or some other label that their manager would never think to question or challenge.

Therefore, contracting and timing are critical, but then, aren't they always?

Projective coaching techniques have the potential to reveal information which the client believes they had hidden from the world. As I'm sure you realise, they are only hiding it from themselves – everyone else knows. The reason that people don't point out your secrets is that they're afraid that you"ll point out theirs in return. That, and the simple fact that nobody cares, they've got their own problems to worry about. As a coach, you do have access to some useful tools, however the most important way in which you add value to your clients is through your external, neutral perspective. The techniques in this book enable you to share that perspective in way that is more gentle and more revealing than the use of coaching questions.

I'll return to the subject of stories in an upcoming chapter, for now you can consider that pictures are a useful projective tool in two ways; firstly as a tool for you to present to the client in order for them to make meaning, and secondly as a way to interpret the pictures that your clients already use to communicate their inner reality.

As a result of reading this chapter, I imagine that you will immediately check what you've been posting in your social media accounts, and wonder what others really make of that.

Are you sharing reality, or an illusion? Or a bit of both? There is no harm in that at all, just as long as you can still tell which is which.

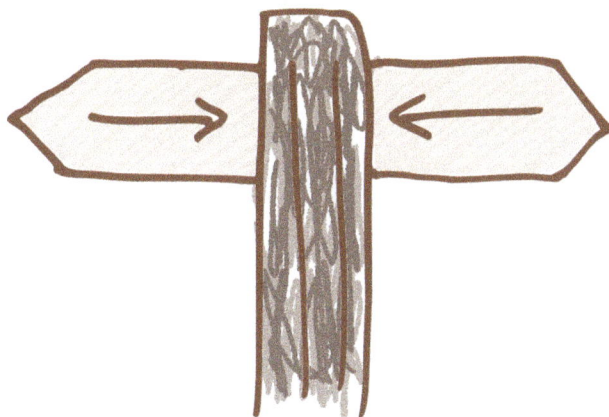

Cards

You will need: Projective cards of your choice

mybook.li/pcc

Today, there are countless different types of projective cards available. The obvious examples are divinatory cards such as tarot cards and their cousins. You can also buy cards to use with various coaching methodologies, psychometric tools, training systems and more.

Archetype cards show a range of possible character types, and their purpose is to show you a set of mirrors for your own personality or situation. You might feel a connection with some, others might make you feel challenged, others might not seem to fit at all. What these cards do is to provoke conversation and reveal connections.

Games cards either feature practice text only or are a regular set of playing cards with some additional text or images to help you learn. For example, you can buy coaching cards that help you to practice useful coaching questions. You can either use them like flashcards, or you can play any card game and invite players to think about or practice what's on each card as they play it.

As you can no doubt see, games cards are not projective, so I will turn to a more detailed discussion of archetype cards.

Strengths-based tools use archetypes to define a person's strengths. There are a number of such systems, listing up to 92 different strengths that a person might possess. The idea is that you rate yourself against the list of strengths and determine which of them you feel least and most strongly connected to. By listing how strongly you feel decisive, creative or polite, the remarkable tool reveals how decisive, creative or polite you are. You can also have your manager or colleagues rate you, which sounds more fun than it really is.

The most famous archetype cards are undoubtedly tarot cards, which date back around 500 years or so. They probably emerged as a card game, and some of them, known as the 'minor arcana', do bear a striking resemblance to traditional Spanish playing cards. Later, the 'major arcana' cards were added which tell the story of our journey through life. The symbolism of tarot cards is well documented in many books and websites, which means that you can either ask your client how they relate to the published symbolism, or you can ask your client to look at the card and notice what they make of it. The most popular and well known tarot cards are the Rider-Waite deck with artwork created in 1910 by Pamela Colman Smith. The Rider-Waite copyright position means that you will find many other tarot designs, with greatly differing images and symbolism, all of which relate in some way to the traditional meanings of the cards.

The purpose of these cards is not to tell you what will happen, but to provide you with a point of reference with which to make sense of your choices in life. Read the card descriptions, look at the imagery and symbolism in the card and consider the questions posed. To what extent does each card resonate with you? What aspect of your personality or situation is the card highlighting?

By choosing cards at random, a person can gain insights into where they are on life's journey. The cards don't tell the future, and they don't reveal hidden secrets, instead they provide a point of reference that you can agree or disagree with. Let's look at three of them by way of demonstration.

The Hermit

This shows the need to spend some time contemplating what is wanted out of life and to start planning ahead. An important decision lies ahead. The Hermit shows the way forward. Follow a spiritual path and learn to trust the answer to all is already within. Meditate.

The symbolism in the card shows a hermit, alone on top of a mountain. He carries a staff to steady himself, so he is going somewhere, and a lantern, which illuminates his path for only a short distance ahead. The hermit is not stuck in a cave, but he is travelling alone, and is only aware of the path immediately in front of him. He has to use trust and intuition to continue on his journey.

Consider your current position in your work or personal relationships.

In what way are you hiding?

Are you taking time to contemplate and reflect?

Are you avoiding anything?

Do you feel at a crossroads, or at least at a point where you could choose different directions?

As you look ahead, does the future seem unclear?

What is your source of strength in this?

What gives you confidence to continue on this path?

What does the Hermit tell you about your own situation?

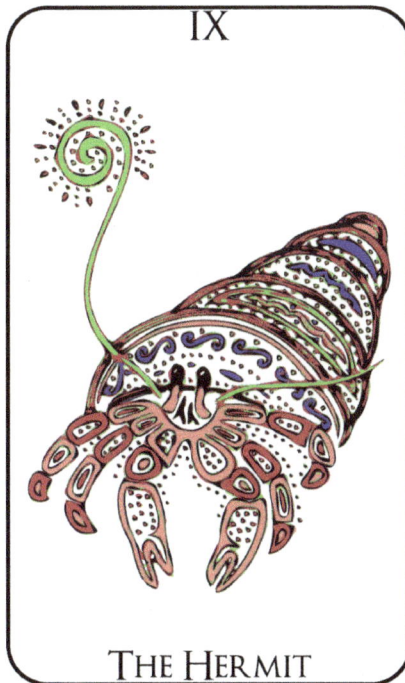

THE HERMIT

The Hanged Man

Life in the balance, this card often means a person is hanging in limbo, can't go back or move forward. Good things to come after adversity. Things are stagnating and feels like nothing will ever change but there is a turning point to come soon.

The symbolism in the card shows a man hanging from a branch. The branch bears leaves, showing that the tree is living. The man's hands are tied behind his back, showing us that he is powerless. Only one foot is tied to the branch, so he is partly free to move. He sees the world from an upside-down perspective. The halo round his head shows us his insight and new knowledge.

Consider your current position in your work or personal relationships.

What in your life feels like it's on 'pause' right now?

In what situations are you waiting for something?

Is there an area of your work or life where you feel powerless?

In what ways are you acting as if you are trapped, when that isn't really the case?

In what ways does your world seem upside down?

How would it be useful to see things from a different perspective?

What insights and knowledge have you gained recently?

Where is the new growth in your life right now?

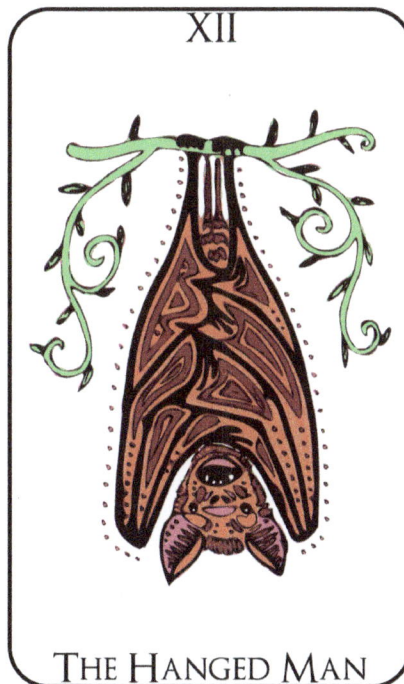

XII

THE HANGED MAN

The Star

The Star of Hope. Optimism and good luck in abundance. After a difficult time things will go very well. Recovery from illness and general good fortune in jobs, relationships and all other areas of life. Often connected to travel and beneficial education. Life enhancing experiences on the way.

A woman is pouring water from two jugs, one in her left hand (unconscious) and one in her right (conscious). Water flows onto the ground in five streams (the five senses). With one foot on the ground (practicality) and the other in the water (intuition) her nakedness shows her vulnerability. In the sky, we see one large star (brilliance and energy) and seven smaller stars (the chakras).

Consider your current position in your work or personal relationships.

What difficult situations in your work or home life are resolving and turning brighter?

What have you learned or achieved from any difficulties that you have recently experienced?

What qualities do you possess which will enable you to shine in the most difficult of circumstances?

How are you using both your practical knowledge and your intuition to be at your best?

How is your vulnerability a strength?

How are you allowing your brilliance to shine?

XVII

THE STAR

Projective Coaching Cards

mybook.li/pcc

I've designed a set of projective coaching cards to accompany this book which you can find by visiting:

projective.coach

The cards feature original photography and can be used in any of the projective coaching methods outlined in the introduction of this book. Here are some ideas:

Associative: Look at random cards and say what feelings or experiences the images bring to mind.

Completion: Look at random images and say what happens next.

Constructive: Select cards and form them into a story.

Ordering: Take a group of cards and order them according to criteria relevant to the topic the client is exploring.

Expressive: Select cards that tell an aspect of the client's life story or current situation.

Relational: Organise a set of cards in relation to the client's current situation.

Here are a few examples of images that you'll find on the cards. There are 5 sets and each set contains 72 cards.

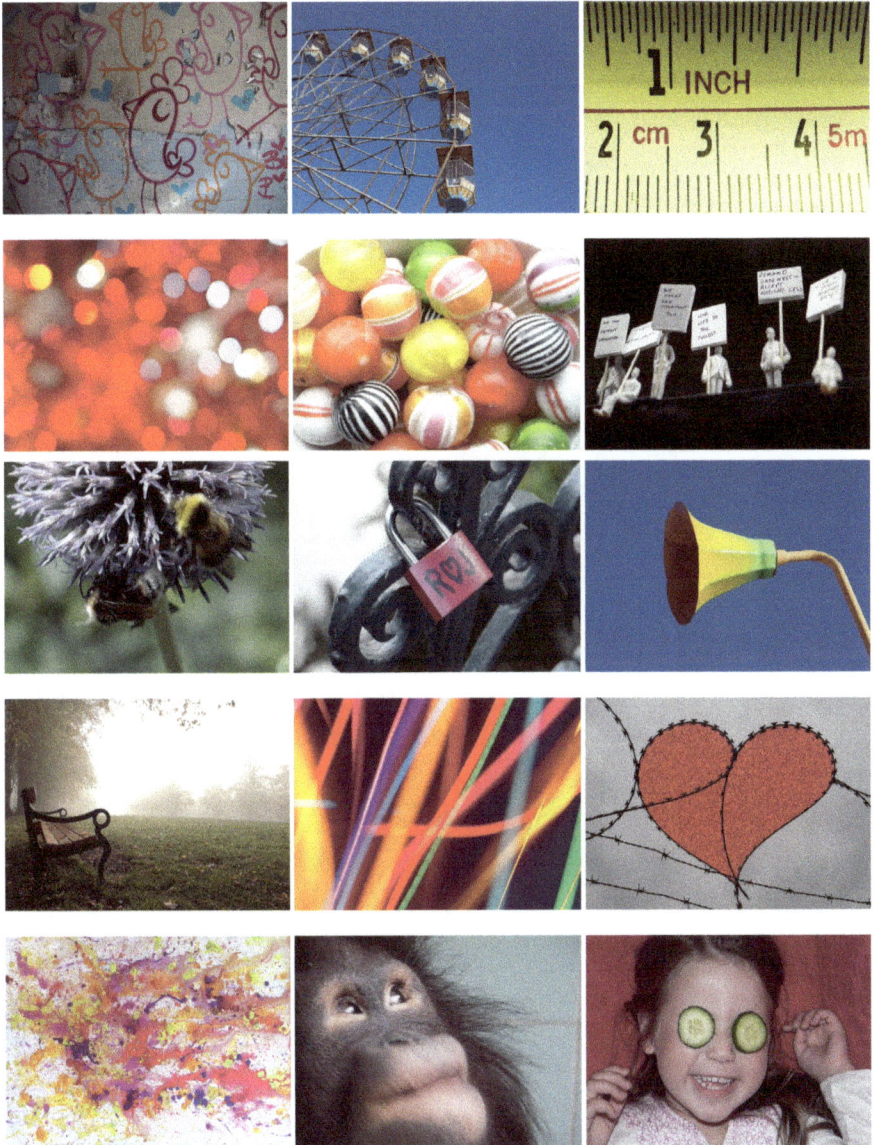

Of course, you can use any suitable cards for this purpose. When I first started to develop projective techniques back in the early 2000s, I had a set of photographs printed for the same purpose. Many of the original images from those photographs are reproduced in the cards that I have created to accompany this book.

You'll also find other sets of projective cards. Find a set that appeals to you and you'll find yourself using it more often.

The whole point of using abstract cards is that they do not intrinsically mean anything, and so there is no limit to the number of ways in which to use them. However, I will share some ideas with you here in more detail.

If you want to try these out quickly, you'll find a random image generator at mybook.li/pcri which features 101 images from across the 5 sets of Projective Coaching Cards.

Associative

Choose six cards at random and arrange them in three groups of pairs.

How have you paired the cards?

What does your chosen criteria tell you that is relevant for you in your life at the moment?

What events in your own life are described by the three pairs of cards?

What do you learn from this?

Relational

Choose three cards at random and take a moment to study the images on them.

Which one most closely represents how you feel right now? And which one is least relevant?

What does the least relevant image reveal about what has been on your mind lately?

What does this mean to you?

Constructive

Consider a current situation in your life which you would like to explore.

Choose three cards at random and create a story which links the three images to your chosen situation.

What do you notice about your story?

Where are you within the story?

What has been edited out of the story?

What does all of this mean for you?

Expressive

Look through the set of cards and choose one card which most clearly expresses what you would really like to say at the moment.

What is preventing you from saying this?

Completion

Choose one card at random. What happens next?

How is that relevant to an issue which is on your mind at the moment?

What would you like to do next?

Ordering

Choose five cards from the set which seem to stand out to you in some way.

Think of something which is very important for you at the moment, such as a value, principle or belief.

Arrange the cards in order, based on which cards least and most represent your chosen value, principle or belief.

How does this help you to stay true to yourself?

Questions and Stories

Coaches are trained to ask questions. One organisation even requires that coaches "ask powerful questions" in order to qualify for membership. This puts a huge pressure on the coach, and hides an important problem with coaching in general, which is that asking questions is often completely counter-productive. Well, at least from the client's point of view. From the point of view of the coach, and therefore the people who make money out of selling certificates to coaches, it's a perfect crime. The coach thinks that their value is in asking questions so that the client finds their own solutions, not realising that asking questions is often what prevents the client from finding a solution. If you have spent a lot of money on coaching training then you might feel offended by this assertion, so I will explain.

When a client describes their current situation to you, they are creating a context. That context then limits the questions you will ask. You might say that a good coach is skilled at getting the client to look past the boundaries of their current situation, but even by thinking that, you are acknowledging that their current situation has boundaries.

I've heard many coaches say that a good question to ask when a client says "I don't know" is "And if you did know, what would the answer be". This is a terrible question! For a start, the coaches who said this couldn't explain *why* they thought it was a good question, they had been told to use it during their coaching training. If you're wondering what's wrong with it then there are two points to consider. First, why are you asking this question? In fact, why are you asking any question? Focus on your intention, not on the clever wording of your questions. Second, you are interpreting the phrase "I don't know" incorrectly. The phrase in itself contains no relevant information, so in your mind, you expand the client's response to fill in the gaps. You act as if the client said "I don't know the answer to that question", but that isn't what the client said, and it's not what they meant either, and if you're about to tell me that I don't know what they meant then neither do you. Before you challenge their response, first get them to complete the sentence at the very least.

Possible expanded statements include:

"I don't know how to put it into words"

"I don't know if I want to tell you"

"I don't know how this is going to make me sound"

When you respond without expanding the client's incomplete sentence with the formulaic "And if you did know, what would the answer be" then you are introducing a new idea, namely that the client doesn't know the answer. "And if you did know" presupposes that the client doesn't know, and "what would the answer be?" presupposes that what the client doesn't know is the answer. It's as if the client says, "I don't know" and the coach says, "That's right, you don't".

There is no merit in arguing "But that's not what the client *means*" or "But that's not what the coach *means*" because in order to understand what someone means that they didn't say, you have to add in new information which was not originally there, which causes the coach to impose their reality onto the client, which completely defeats the object of asking questions in the first place. The coach could save everyone some valuable time and just say, "You don't know what you're doing so I'm going to tell you".

I'm greatly in favour of a coach asking questions, and it's certainly more valuable in many cases than the coach simply telling the client what to do, no matter how obvious that solution may be. My point is that the coach must understand *why* they are asking a particular question. As I've said, first clarify your intention and only then come up with a question. Asking a question to fill an awkward silence or to get the client talking is not a useful intention. All too often, I have met coaches who ask questions because they've been taught to ask questions, not because they understand *why* they're asking questions. They've been taught that asking questions is non-directive, and the value of a coach is in helping the client to discover their own answers.

The promise of 'non-directive coaching' sounds like a nice ideal, but in practice it's impossible to achieve. Every question you ask is directive, because every question you ask gets the client to think about something that they would not otherwise have thought about. Even a gentle nudge such as, "Can you tell me more about that?" is directive, because up until that point, the client had told you precisely what they wanted to tell you. By asking them to tell you more, you're now directing them to tell you something that they had previously chosen not to tell you.

Whether you think you can get your client to think outside the box or not, you are accepting the client's reality, and the box that contains it. Any question that you ask your client is constrained by the situation that they have described to you. The problem with this, as described in my book Coaching Excellence, is that the client isn't telling you the truth about their current situation – they are telling you precisely what they want you to know, so that you do only what they want you to do.

The solution that I am proposing to you is non-contextual questioning. The problem with coaching questions is that they are a contextual response to something the client has said, and are therefore constrained by the client's linguistic map of their reality. The coach has to work very hard indeed to introduce the possibility of change, because every question that the coach asks accepts the status quo, in that every question accepts the client's preceding statement as true. In order to introduce the possibility of change, the coach has to introduce something which isn't in the client's linguistic map, and to do that whilst asking questions which are constrained by the topic of conversation is tricky.

Non-contextual questions neither accept nor reject the client's reality. In the next chapter, I'll share a non-contextual coaching tool with you; The Unsticker. Because the questions, at least in The Unsticker, are generated randomly, they cannot have any contextual relationship to the client's story. And yet, because the questions are asked within a conversation about the client's story, there must logically be a relationship.

Another important distinction is that a coach's usual questions are asked in expectation of a contextually relevant answer, and that answer will constrain the next question. Therefore, a series of questions within a coaching session will tend to narrow the scope for the client's responses, which is of course highly directive. Non-contextual questions seem to have the opposite effect. Each question neither relies on the preceding response nor constrains the next question, and the effect tends to broaden the scope of the conversation.

So if the questions are random and therefore unconnected to the client's story, but asking the questions implies that they must be connected, how does the client resolve this conflict?

Simply, in order to make sense of the question, the client must change the way they think about the problem. The random presentation of the questions means that the coach cannot impose any agenda other than to shift the client's thinking. Where they shift to is entirely up to them.

The questions are designed to present options which are unlikely to apply to the client's problem. Unless the problem is already a cake, the client is very unlikely to have considered what kind of cake it is. Yet to answer that question, the client must organise their perception in such a way as to compare it with the qualities that a cake may have. The client is led to reorganise the problem, or at least to reorganise the relationships that create the problem, in a way which would not be possible if you asked the client directly to consider an alternative perspective.

Imagine that you have a problem at work, something that is frustrating you. Imagine that you talk to a friend about the problem. Your friend will ask questions about the situation at work, and they will present you with neat solutions, such as, "You need to tell your boss where to stick his job", or, "You should make a complaint to HR", or, "You should demand a pay rise for all that extra hassle!"

How do you respond to this advice? With rejections such as, "Yeah, but...", or, You don't understand", or, "I've tried that already, nothing works", or just a half hearted, "Yeah, maybe".

What this demonstrates is that your critical filter is working perfectly. From an early age, you learned to create an abstract map of reality, and you then learned to protect that map from the influence of others. Your concept of how the world works became fixed and hard to change. This is when you learned that your thoughts are private and are not shared in other peoples' heads, and based on that insight, you learned to lie, which is an important defensive skill.

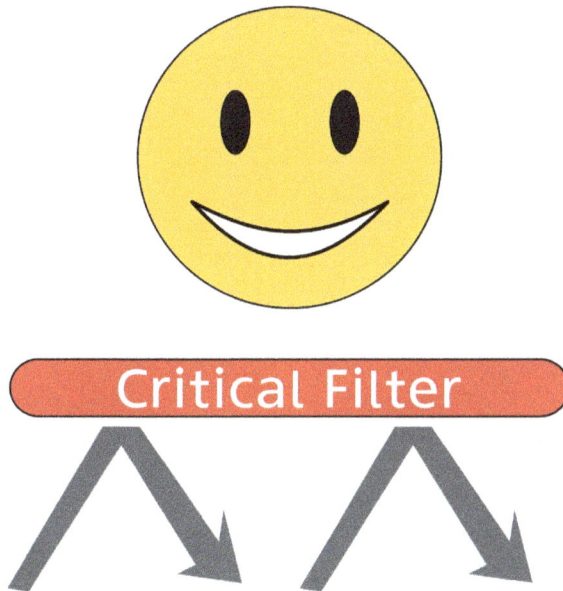

The critical filter will automatically intercept any form or structure of communication which sounds like someone is trying to tell you what to think, feel or do.

You might associate this most strongly with your teenage years, however that's a slightly different process which is known as 'individuation'. That's more about social rules than your view of the world. The much earlier process of creating your abstract map of reality takes place at what is called the 'Pre-operational stage' of neurological development, and this takes place between 2 and 7 years of age. One of the best-known developmental tests at this stage is Piaget's 'mountain range'.

Jean Piaget called this the ability to 'decentre', which he investigated with the following experiment.

Piaget sat down at a table with a model mountain range on it. He asked a child to tell him which view of the mountain range Piaget could see. Younger children indicated their own point of view, older children indicated Piaget's point of view, demonstrating their ability to see the model from an imaginary angle.

Here is a top view of a version of Piaget's mountain range (two balls and a cube) showing the positions of Piaget and a child.

Which of the following views would the child see, and which would Piaget see?

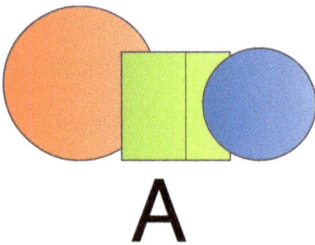

A

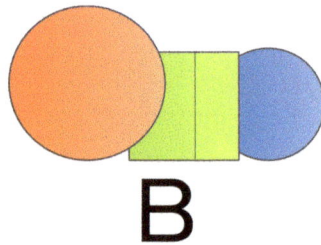

B

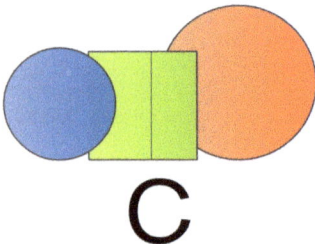

C

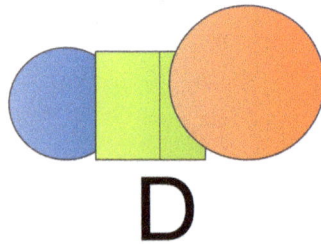

D

This ability to see things from another person's point of view is of course an example of projection, and it's something that we do whenever we empathise with another person.

There are two simple ways to bypass the critical filter, using two simple communication forms which you will already be very familiar with – questions and stories.

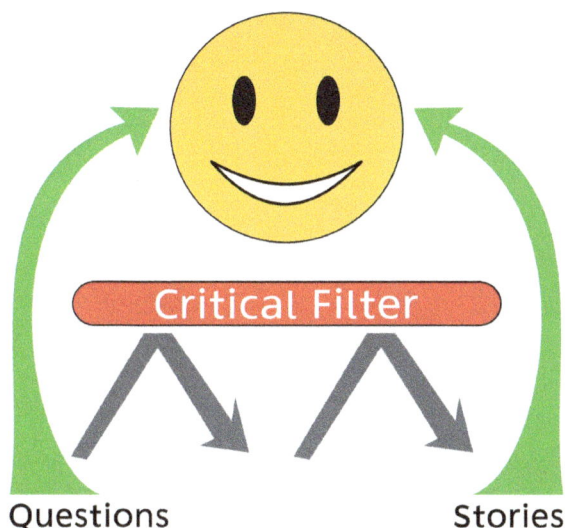

A question doesn't convey information or instruction, so you don't have to protect yourself from its influence.

However, every question contains a dangerous payload known as a presupposition, which is the concept which must be held true in order for the question to make sense.

For example, if I ask you, "Have you seen my new car" then I presuppose that a car exists, that it is new, and that you may or may not have seen it. While you're busy focusing on the 'seen' part, the 'new car' part slips past your critical filter.

Let's consider a more insidious example. "Do you know what time the meeting about the reorganisation is?"

No? Oh, didn't you know? Weren't you invited?

The presupposition contained within every question means that your intention is revealed in the questions that you ask. I'm sure that you're a very good coach, and you recognise the difference between a question designed to explore, and a question designed to manoeuvre your client round to your way of thinking. Therefore you would never ask a question like, "Have you thought about…?", or, "What if you…?", or, "Do you think it might be a good idea to…?", because you would recognise those as deliberately leading questions. If you've got a suggestion to make, make it. If the client disagrees, they can disagree. When you hide the suggestion within a question, they might not have the conscious choice to disagree. More dangerously, you might not realise you're doing it, and you might not realise that you've stopped coaching your client and lapsed into coaching yourself.

Stories slip right past the critical filter because you can listen to a story without having to agree or disagree with it, without having to judge it as true or false. You can put yourself into the story, you can even empathise with the characters and feel what they might be feeling.

You'll recognise some projective techniques categories as being story-based, including Completion, Constructive and Expressive. The idea in the basic form of these techniques is that a story which seems abstract is actually a metaphor for a personal experience. For example, if you used the pictures from the Pictures chapter and asked your client to tell a story about the giraffe, he or she might talk about a baby giraffe who had lost its mother, or a giraffe that overcame a problem to find its friends, or a giraffe that was very happy and respected by other animals. The giraffe is not experiencing any of these things. If you're thinking that a giraffe might not experience respect but it can certainly lose its mother then you have fallen into the trap of the story. The giraffe does not exist. It's just a picture in a book.

A story can exist within a single sentence, if we define a story as being a sequence of events taking place either not here, or not now, or not to you.

To make sense of the story, whether it be a film, a book or an account of your friend's recent holiday, you put yourself into the mind of the character that you most identify with, or which the author or director wants you to identify with. You are able to do this because you know the story is not about you, so there is no need to protect yourself from influence. However, as soon as you identify with a character and project yourself into the story, it becomes about you. A story is therefore able to convey concepts, ideas, emotions and opinions into your mind without your conscious awareness or intervention. Throughout history, the creators of political propaganda have known this, and used this to create books and films that told a story from one point of view, that "we" are good, and "they" are evil and must be stopped. The problem is that the boundaries between good and evil are rather grey, and the differences between them and us are rather arbitrary, and prone to change.

In order to project yourself into a story, you must be able to connect some feature of a character in the story with something you attribute to yourself. For example, in the biblical story of David and Goliath, which character are you?

I'm guessing that because you don't like to think of yourself as an aggressive, bullying behemoth, you chose David, the plucky young underdog.

What I have found is that people have a life story which plays out a familiar scene, over and over again. Some people will always identify with the abandoned child, or the underdog, or the person who wins against all odds. These stories are neither true nor false in themselves, yet they become part of our life narrative.

I've also found a surprisingly easy way to identify these stories, and reveal the narrative that defines a person's life.

Think of a scene in a film, TV series or book which always creates a strong emotional response in you. Maybe it brings a tear to your eye, or you feel a sudden up-swell of anger or pride. Think of a few scenes that have this effect for you.

Here are a few examples submitted by readers – do watch out for spoilers!

Avengers Endgame: The funeral of Tony Stark.

Dumbo: His mother reaches through the bars of the cage and puts her trunk around him.

The Perks of Being a Wallflower: On being an outsider.

Naruto: Jiraiya dies, fulfilling his role in the prophecy.

Doctor Strange: The Ancient One says, "It's not about you".

Cinderella Man: James Braddock gets knocked down, sees the image of his children starving and picks himself up.

Guardians of the Galaxy 2: Yondu sacrifices himself to save Peter, saying, "He may have been your father, boy, but he wasn't your daddy."

Gladiator: Maximus talks about the loss of his family.

The Champ: The boy is fighting with the realisation that an invincible father figure is not an immortal care giver.

Kingsman The Golden Circle: Merlin steps on the landmine.

Apollo 13: The return after the communication blackout.

Battlestar Galactica (2003 TV series): Adama stages a daring return to New Caprica to rescue the people previously abandoned and subsequently imprisoned by the Cylons.

The Graduate: The lovers get on the bus at the end and Dustin Hoffman smiles.

Seven: The box arrives.

Saving Private Ryan: "I've already lost two sons…".

Les Miserables: "Bring him home".

The Matrix: Neo's reincarnation.

Brave: "Mend the bond".

Marley and Me: The dog dies.

Harry Potter and the Philosopher's Stone: Harry sees his parents in the Mirror of Erised.

Cranford: Grieving parents are looking for their lost son.

Facing the Giants: A player succeeds in a demanding physical task that he did not believe he could complete.

The Shawshank Redemption: Red walks up to Andy on the beach.

Gone with the Wind: Scarlett says, "After all, tomorrow is another day!"

The Prince of Tides: Tom visits Susan to tell her he's going back to his wife.

Star Wars The Empire Strikes Back: Leia says "I love you" as Han Solo is about to be imprisoned, and he replies, "I know".

Toy Story 3: Woody takes Buzz's hand in the incinerator.

Naruto: Itachi sacrifices himself for honour and teaching.

Good Will Hunting: "It's not your fault."

In Which We Serve: "Remember the Torrin".

Ae Watan: In a song about loyalty, every child in the class interprets the words according to their own perspective.

Dirty Dancing: "Me?. I'm scared of everything. I'm scared of what I saw, I'm scared of what I did, about who I am and most of all I'm scared of walkin' out of this and never feelin' the rest of my whole life the way I feel when I'm with you."

The Matrix: Smith describes the human race as a virus.

The Railway Children: "Daddy, my Daddy!"

The Matrix: Morpheus speaks to the people of Zion.

Gone with the Wind: "Frankly my dear, I don't give a damn."

Jerry McGuire: "You had me at hello".

Coach Carter: "Our deepest fear is not that we are inadequate, our deepest fear is that we are powerful beyond measure."

Avengers Endgame: "We're going to be OK. You can rest now."

Star Wars The Rise of Skywalker: Rey buries the lightsabers.

Dirty Dancing: "No-one puts baby in a corner" and her father stands up for her.

The Bridge on the River Kwai: Colonel Nicholson turns on his own allies to protect his bridge.

The Impossible: Henry phones home.

In Which We Serve: A telegram arrives; Shorty is safe.

Toy Story 3: Lotso smashes Big Baby's name tag.

Wall-E. Eve repairs Wall-E but he doesn't remember her.

The Shawshank Redemption: Red says, "Get busy living, or get busy dying".

It seems from the responses from my family, friends and colleagues that I could fill an entire book just with scenes that trigger powerful emotional responses. Of course, they are designed specifically to do that, so this in itself is not a surprise. What I do find interesting is that everyone I ask can immediately connect a list of personally significant film scenes with events in their own life story, starting with an emotionally charged event from their childhood. That same scene then seems to repeat throughout life. Can this really be a coincidence? Or is it possible that we are each recreating these scenes for a purpose?

My working theory is that an event occurs in childhood which is perceived as a fundamental injustice. For the rest of that person's life, they are driven to right that wrong, to restore justice. However, they cannot turn back the clock, and so they continue to seek out or create situations in which they project that injustice forwards, giving them temporary satisfaction but never undoing what was done so long ago.

To have a sense of justice, two factors must be present; a comparison to a perceived equal, and an authority figure or arbiter. Imagine the situation where one sibling gets to stay up late and watch TV, the younger one does not. What does the younger sibling say?

"It's not fair"

What does this have to do with projective coaching?

Remember Piaget's mountain range experiment. One of the most important examples of projection is our ability to project our mind into the mind of another person, to see the world from their point of view, to experience their choices in the context of their life. As a coach, you are no doubt well-trained in the discipline of being non-judgemental. I am sure that you apply this principle effortlessly to your clients. Do you apply it equally to yourself?

A child sees the world around them, but they do not so easily see themselves in that context. They are very aware of the behaviour of others, yet they are much less aware of the reasons for that behaviour. Play the story forwards a few years and you might find yourself getting annoyed by a slow driver without stopping to think about why they are driving so slowly. And when your boss snaps at you, is your first thought based on empathy of the pressure that they might be under, or is it based on the injustice of their terse response to your question?

As a coach, you help your client to explore these temporary reactions and to view the situation from multiple positions in order to gain a more complete understanding of why things are the way that they are. Asking your client to imagine how things look from their boss's point of view is an obvious example of projective coaching. If you're wondering where this fits into the six main categories of projective techniques, I suspect that it doesn't really fit at all, but it is closest to the role playing example of an Expressive technique, because in order to role play being someone else, you have to perform a projective mind read. My reason for including it in the book is that it's an interesting application of a person's natural ability to place their mind into another person or an inanimate object or a brush and paint or the words of a song. Whilst the projective techniques presented here are highly valuable, don't overlook the most commonplace projection of all.

With this in mind, you can begin to combine projective techniques. For example, you might have your client draw three circles, and then have them draw what they think their manager might draw. You could then explore the differences between the two diagrams, and the implications for your client's relationship with their manager.

One of the ways in which I use projective techniques with corporate groups is to have the team members work alone in the first stage and then combine what they have created and then work collectively.

For example, if the members of a team draw their experience of working in the team then I would join all of the drawings together and have them add to the whole to represent the team as they would like it to be in the future. Individuals can talk about their own drawings as a way of expressing their feelings and experiences, and then collaborate to create a sense of inclusivity. It can be a very gentle way to recognise individual positions and then incorporate those positions into a sense of collective authority. Fundamentally, every member of a team wants to feel both part of and apart from the team at the same time. Each person wants to belong, to have a sense of safety and community, and at the same time to be recognised and valued as an individual. Projective techniques provide you with many ways to facilitate this.

To return to the essence of this chapter, questions and stories are, in themselves, valuable projective techniques. The questions that a person asks reveal their internal reality and their agenda, and the stories they tell reveal their attempts to impose that reality onto others. By sharing stories, and by creating shared stories, we create new realities, with all of the opportunities that they may bring.

The Unsticker

You will need:

A problem that makes you feel stuck

Optional – an Android smartphone or iPhone

mybook.li/pcus

The Unsticker is an amazing problem solving tool. If your client feels stuck, simply ask them random questions and after just a few minutes, their problem will change, or they will have forgotten what it was.

This is a short set of 99 questions, the same set as you'll find in the book Coaching Excellence. In the free smartphone app, there are 200, and in The Unsticker book, there are over 300.

I mentioned earlier that The Unsticker contains all six types of projective technique, presented for you as a fun problem solving tool which generates random questions.

As you look through the list of questions, you will see how these different techniques are hidden within the structure of the question. Here are some examples:

Associative   What time is the problem?

Completion   What will you do?

Constructive What does this problem mean?

Ordering   Is the problem half full or half empty?

Expressive   Imagine a child had this problem. What is your advice to them?

Relational   Is the problem near or far?

As you look at the structure of the questions, you'll see that there are also linguistic tricks which don't fit into these six categories, and so the questions are not purely projective. For example, 'How does the problem look through the wrong end of a telescope?' causes the client to visualise the problem as smaller. This changes the sensory perception of the problem. The overall effect of all of the questions presented to the client is relational, in that the problem is not, itself, the problem. The problem, as the client describes it, is a set of perceived relationships. The problem does not 'exist' in the objective world, it is entirely subjective, and is therefore created as a set of sensory distortions which exist in the relationships between the elements of the problem. The client, in creating the problem, does not include all possible elements, they only include the elements which support their assertion that this situation constitutes a problem.

For example, imagine that your washing machine is broken, such that it no longer heats the water. It does everything else as you would expect. Is this a problem? From one point of view, yes. From another, the washing machine is now improved; it is more energy efficient.

Even if you view this situation as a problem, the problem does not exist within the washing machine. If you have no need to do any washing then there's no problem. The scale of the problem increases as your washing basket gets fuller and your sock drawer gets emptier. Therefore, the problem is not the faulty washing machine, the problem is the lack of clean clothes, and even that is relative to what you define as clean, and how many times you might be comfortable wearing the same pair of socks.

The structure of The Unsticker's questions force the client to change the relationships between these various elements, transforming the situation from a problem into something else. The washing machine still needs to be repaired, but it's no longer a problem, just something that needs to be done.

You might have felt that 'force' was a strong word, because you've been trained to believe that the client always has choice, and can choose to answer a question or not. This is not true, because the really clever part of The Unsticker is that the client does not need to answer the question in order for the tool to work – they only need to hear the question, and unless they leave the room, they have no choice over whether to hear it or not. Therefore, as a coach, you cannot ask a non-directive question, and you cannot allow your client the choice to answer or not, because the power of the question comes when it is asked, not when it is answered.

The Unsticker is a handy, ready-made example of something that I have named 'non-contextual questioning' and as a coaching intervention, it can be extremely powerful.

Non-contextual questions alone will have some effect, but when the questions contain linguistic structures that lead to different perspectives and perceptions, the effect is much more powerful. For example, if I ask you how big a problem is, that creates a different perception compared with if I ask you what size the problem is, or how small the problem is. It is so easy for a coach to lead the client with their language that the coach really can't avoid imposing their own reality. The use of a random set of questions completely separates the coaching relationship from the coach's expectations and agenda. The use of such carefully structured non-contextual questions therefore causes the client to change their perception in a way that that coach can't predict or control.

What is most interesting is the relevance of the client's answers to these questions. As I mentioned, the next question is independent of the preceding answer, but more than that, the client's answer is completely irrelevant. Their answer is of course very relevant for them, and may have an emotional resonance which they had not expected, yet it is irrelevant for the coach in that the coach does not make any use of the answer and therefore doesn't even need to hear it. In some situations, the client may prefer not to answer the questions, instead indicating that they are ready for the next.

What this reveals is potentially the most powerful aspect of The Unsticker – that in order for the questions to change the client's perspective and behaviour, the client does not need to answer the questions. The client only needs to hear the questions for them to have their effect, because it is not the creation of an answer which reframes the problem, it is the processing of the question itself. By the time the client has heard the question, it has already changed the problem.

Imagine the influence you can have with that one fact.

Using The Unsticker is very easy; simply think of a problem, try to hold it firmly in your mind, then ask random questions until the problem changes. The questions are numbered so that you can generate random numbers in order to choose questions. If you choose questions by sticking your finger in the book, or choosing what seem like random questions, you'll probably end up only asking questions from around the middle of the list. You can use a random number generator, such as the one built into Google search, or the one at www.random.org, both of which allow you to set an upper and lower limit and then generate a sequence of numbers.

It's very important that you ask the question chosen. If you look at a question and think, "Oh, not that one, let's look for a better one" then the questions are not random, and you are biasing the result. Even if you don't like the question, ask it, otherwise you are making the question fit the problem, and it will be ineffective.

You can find the free smartphone app versions of The Unsticker by following these links.

Android: mybook.li/pcua

Apple: mybook.li/pcui

You can find an online version of The Unsticker here:

theunsticker.com

1   What is it that you don't want to happen?

2   When was this problem past its 'best before' date?

3   Are you secretly in love with this problem?

4   Do you need anyone else to do this for you?

5   When will you have solved this problem yet?

6   So what?

7   Is the problem colourful or grey?

8   What do you want most of all?

9   What would happen if you didn't?

10 Is the problem somewhere, everywhere, nowhere or anywhere?

11 Where would this problem be without you?

12 Who can you turn to?

13 If your problem was a movie, who would play the problem?

14 How do you know?

15 How does the problem look in a mirror?

16 If you turned this problem on its head, how would it smell?

17 Is the problem half full or half empty?

18 What would happen if you deflated the problem a little more?

19 What time is the problem?

20 Does the problem sink or float?

21 How does the problem look on fast forward?

22 What will you do?

23 In a TV talent show, how far would the problem get?

24 How is the problem going?

25 How does the problem look through the wrong end of a telescope?

26 What mustn't you do?

27 How slow is this problem?

28 Is the problem warm or cool?

29 What happens when you turn the sound down on the problem?

30 Which superhero would have this problem as an arch enemy?

31 What would happen if you did?

32 What sizes does your problem come in?

33 What would it be like to fly the problem like a kite?

34 Do you enjoy the attention you get from having had this problem?

35 Are you certain this is your problem?

36 Is the problem near or far?

37 How would a baker roll out the problem?

38 How does this problem help you?

39 If this problem were a shop, what shop would it be?

40 Is the problem lighter at the top or at the bottom?

41 Is the problem wrapped in aluminium foil or cling film?

42 What stops you from doing what you have already decided to do?

43 How would a gangster deal with the problem?

44 When did you first know about this?

45 Is the problem here or there?

46 What have you done to earn this problem?

47 If you wrap yourself up in a warm duvet, how does the problem feel?

48 What kind of cloud would this problem make?

49 What would you do?

50 If this problem were a fruit, what fruit would it be?

51 Has the problem's fuse blown?

52 Is the problem tied up with string or ribbon?

53 Is the problem ripe yet?

54 When you look back on this problem, what will make you laugh most?

55 If this problem were a vegetable, what vegetable would it be?

56 What would you do if you could?

57 If you painted this problem, which colour would you use third?

58 If you look at the problem through a microscope, what do you see?

59 What happens if you turn the brightness of the problem up?

60 What will you do differently next time?

61 How does the problem sound at the wrong speed?

62 What does this problem taste like?

63 What won't you do?

64 How will having had this problem have helped you?

65 Where would this problem hold a tea party?

66 What's the one thing you would like most of all, right now?

67 What would you do if things weren't the same?

68 What kind of cake could solve this problem?

69 Why don't you stop playing with your problem?

70 What shouldn't you do?

71 Is the problem wider at the start or at the end?

72 How has the problem changed tomorrow?

73 When did you first start to think this way?

74 If the problem went to a fancy dress party, what would it dress up as?

75 What does this problem mean?

76 If you close your eyes, how does the problem look?

77 Was this a problem a month ago?

78 How does the problem look on rewind?

79 How would the problem be treated by airport baggage handlers?

80 When did you last worry about this?

81 Did you enjoy the sympathy that this problem got for you?

82 How many 'dislikes' would this problem get on Facebook?

83 Was this a problem a week ago?

84 How could you make money out of this problem?

85 Would the problem go off if you didn't keep it in the fridge?

86 Was this a problem a year ago?

87 When did you last think about this?

88 What colour is this problem?

89 As you see yourself with this problem, what strikes you as odd?

90 Is the problem held together with sticky tape or glue?

91 What kind of animal could solve this problem?

92 What can't you do?

93 Have you looked for the problem's reset button?

94 When do you want this to change?

95 How light is this problem?

96 What if?

97 What are you stopping yourself from doing?

98 Imagine a child had this problem. What is your advice to them?

99 What are you not allowing yourself to think about doing?

The Untangler

mybook.li/pcut

When a problem is too big to think about, you literally 'can't get your head round it'. So if you can't get your head around it, get it out of your head. With a complex problem, it can be very important to get the problem into a format that you can interact with physically.

A complex problem is made up of many elements, and those elements in themselves are not the problem – the problem is the way that those elements are related to each other, and those relationships are created in your subjective reality, and therefore can be changed without having to change any of the 'facts' of the problem.

This is a very good exercise to do alone, and of course you can also use it with a single client or even with a group.

Stage 1: Collecting

First, allow the client to choose a colour for you to use on the cards. Ask them to choose a colour that they would associate with words of great value and importance to them.

Second, ask them to start talking about the situation that they want to explore.

To get your client talking, you might ask for a headline or title for the subject they're going to talk about, and that will be the first word or phrase that you write down.

As your client tells you their story, they will mark out certain words, and your task is to simply write down any words or short phrases which you notice are marked out in some way.

Words will be marked out through non-verbal emphasis, through pauses, through gestures, through repetition, through a change in voice tone and through the use of emotionally charged words.

You might find that your client stops talking after just a few cards. In that case, ask them to continue.

As a guide, around 15 to 20 cards is enough for the client to be able to explore all aspects of the situation from different angles. Any more than that can be overwhelming.

You'll find a video of the stages of the exercise at mybook.li/pcut and you might find that helpful in judging which words to write down, because you can't write down everything your client says, and in any case, if you create more than 20 cards, your client will have so much work to do that the exercise will take all day.

As I mentioned, you can even use this exercise by yourself. Allow yourself to daydream through the problem, thinking about all the different elements or components that contribute to it. Think about all the consequences and factors. Think about all the people involved. Write down all the elements of the problem, along with anything else that seems important onto your cards. Do not try to think in a structured way, it's important that you just allow yourself to daydream.

Stage 2: First layout

When you have a stack of cards, give them to your client and ask them to arrange the cards on the table or floor. They can arrange them however they want and in any order. They are allowed to do anything with the cards that makes sense to them.

When the client has finished, ask them to step back and take some time to notice how the arrangement of cards relates to the situation that they have described.

There's no 'right' or 'wrong' way to arrange the cards, just something that works for the client. As they sort and arrange the cards, a pattern will emerge that is generated by the way they structure this situation in their mind, and the exercise allows them to organise and understand the situation in a way that they can't when thinking about it logically.

After you have given your client some thinking time, you can begin to ask questions about the layout. You might ask questions in the following categories, depending on the way that the client has positioned the cards.

Groups

How have you grouped the cards?

What would you call each of these groups?

What do these cards have in common?

How is the position of the groups important?

Are there any cards which don't fit anywhere?

Are these cards opposing or balancing each other?

Space

What is in the 'empty' space between cards or groups?

Why are these cards touching?

Are these cards or groups being pushed apart or pulled together?

If so, by what force?

If so, what is the source of this force?

Does the space contain any missing cards?

What is important about the space between cards or groups?

Orientation

Are the cards all aligned in the same way?

If the cards are oriented differently, why is that?

Does the orientation of the cards imply movement?

If so, towards or away from?

Regularity

Are the cards grouped neatly?

If some are neat and some not, what is the difference?

Patterns

Do any of the groups form a shape which looks familiar?

If so, how is that connected to the situation?

Does the pattern give any sense of movement?

Step back as far as you can, what does the overall shape remind you of?

Stage 3: Rearrangement

Once you have explored the first layout created by the client, they can begin to make changes. Here are some examples of questions you might ask to get them to think about the meaning of the patterns and what insights they might gain from this.

Now that you have explored the patterns in the cards, are there any cards that you feel don't belong here?

If so, what would you like to do with those cards?

Are there any cards missing?

If so, what cards would you like to create?

Often, you will have cards which don't quite belong, but which the client can't discard either. It's as if the word or phrase on the card has both positive and negative aspects, and the client can't lose one without losing the other. In this instance, you can use a nice trick to separate the card into it's different aspects. Let's call this trick 'Flipping'.

Hold the card up the your client and say something like, "This card shows you something which isn't entirely good and isn't entirely bad, and that makes it hard to make sense of, and what you don't realise yet is that there's something written on the back. When you think about this word from the perspective of it being something useful and valuable, something that you want to hold on to, you'll know what's written on the other side. So in a moment I'm going to turn this card over, and on the reverse you'll see a word which describes the same thing, but is something valuable and worth holding on to." Now, flip the card over and ask the client what word they see. Almost every time, a new word comes immediately to mind which reframes the meaning of the original word into something which has value for the client. Here are some example of the kinds of words pairs that result from flipping:

Original word	Flipped word
Reluctant	Patient
Disorganised	Spontaneous
Anger	Power
Lonely	Alone
Trapped	Safe

Often, I find that the original words are not actually the client's own words, they are words that other people have used to judge their behaviour.

Examples

If you want to see videos of this technique in action, visit mybook.li/pcut.

This example came from someone who was trying to find a way of channelling energy more effectively. The layout of the cards seems to be an equation with the solution being somewhere to the right of the equals sign. The E stood for Energy.

This example came from someone who was planning a career change and needed a clear direction through some problems. As he lay out the cards, names for the three parts of the arrow came to mind. To the left is 'planning', to the right is 'information' and at the top lies 'purpose'.

One card did not fit in the arrow shape and it turned out to represent a problem that this person had been giving himself. He threw the card away and the problem disappeared.

In this next example, the problem was spread all over the table, seeping into all areas of this person's life and having many consequences:

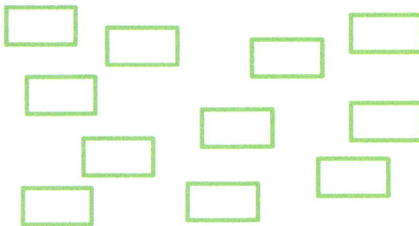

When the problem timeframe was moved into the past, all the cards ended up in one neat pile:

Essentially, this person realised that the problem wasn't a problem at all - in fact, she enjoyed having it! The problem that had spread throughout her life became neatly packed away, correlating with the change in the way she began to think about the pattern of behaviour.

In this next example, the person concerned had a problem connected with public speaking that would cause him considerable stress. In the present, the problem was again spread out, correlating strongly with the way that the problem spread into many areas of his life:

By shifting the problem into the past, it split into two halves. The problem naturally separated into an area that was out of his control and therefore not worth worrying about, and an area that was under his control. This gave him a clear sense of motivation to make specific changes in his life.

The stack of cards on the left represents his emotional state with respect to the problem. The cards on the right represent parts of the problem that are 'real' for him and that he can influence directly.

The next example came from someone who sees time in an arc, with the future stretching away to the right. By moving the problem into the past, the problem split into two separate 'timelines'.

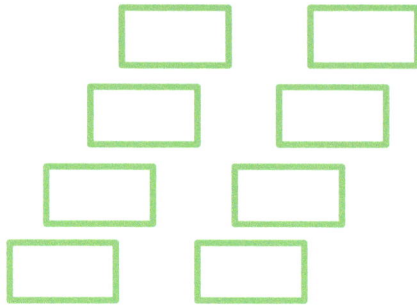

The track on the left is a specific instance of the problem whilst the track on the right represents the 'constant' elements of the problem which are the important lessons to be learned from it. It is very important when solving problems that you learn something useful before discarding them - don't throw the baby out with the bathwater.

Here are a few card layouts that clients came up with during a leadership workshop. The purpose of using the Untangler in this context was to create personal alignment, self-awareness and a sense of purpose, without which it is probably more difficult to lead others.

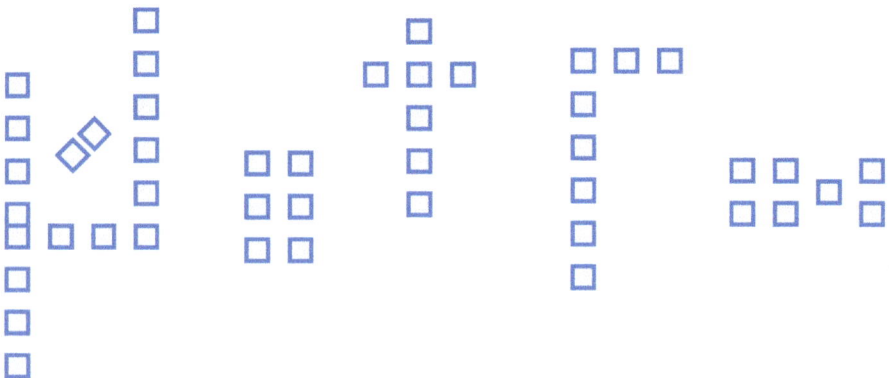

Here are two photos of the process in action. The first photo shows the halfway point, where the layout is visibly open and fragmented. The second photo shows the final pattern.

By exploring the relationships between the groups, we discovered that the client has been putting energy into keeping two aspects of his working life apart. The two cards that you can see in the gap are wedging the pattern open. After exploring these two cards, the pattern quickly resolved into a very symmetrical shape, which had both a strong metaphorical, and a very literal meaning for the client.

When he read through the words on the cards, what he had created was a very neat problem solving process which first expands the problem in order to gather more information and then reduces the problem down to a clear solution.

This is the final pattern. Whilst this is still too complex, it is a good example of progress that the client makes on the way to self-organising around a new set of perceptions and beliefs. This client had felt stuck in his role, and pulled in different directions by work and family responsibilities. This was creating a lot of stress and anxiety for him.

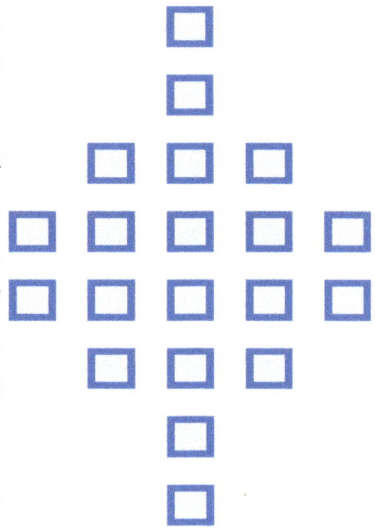

A few months after this exercise, he moved to a new job that enabled him to move back to his home country to bring his family closer together. It seemed that he had become entangled in his own process of trying to balance his priorities and please everyone, and by clarifying all of this, he was able to focus on what was most important.

What this can show you is that you don't have to achieve everything in one coaching session. Sometimes, you only have to introduce a little clarity and the client will do the rest, in their own time. Remember too that the client is part of a system. They have bosses, colleagues, friends and family to consider, and to talk to, in order to make concrete changes in their lives.

One technical manager arranged his cards in a vertical line as shown on the left. When I asked him what the arrangement meant, he said, "I'm an engineer so my cards are in a straight line." I said, "You call yourself an engineer?! You call that a straight line?!"

This can have two meanings. Either what he thinks is acceptable as a straight line is not how others might see it, or he is trying to break free from the straight line, trying to introduce an element of uncertainty into a predictable sequence. His career has been a linear progression, and six months after arranging those cards, he was considering a sideways move for the first time.

You can see that there is no 'right' or 'wrong' way to arrange the cards, only a way that is meaningful to the person with the problem. You can also see the interesting correlation between the layout of the cards and the nature of the problem itself. In all of these examples, the people concerned were as surprised as anyone else to see the chosen layout unfolding in front of them. In each case, the meaning of the layout was obvious and helped the person to create new choices in handling the problem.

A problem such as a flat tyre or broken window isn't going to disappear just because you've moved some cards around. That's not the kind of problem we're talking about. Fortunately, those kinds of problems are very easy to fix, because you know what resources are required. This 'Untangler' exercise is really excellent for problems involving people within systems and relationships, where the problems are not created by physical faults but by relationships, perceptions and assumptions.

When a situation or problem has been churning around in your head for a while, it quickly becomes mixed up with other thoughts, ideas and concerns. As soon as more than one person becomes involved, the situation gets even worse as each person carries a unique and different representation of the problem. Thinking about the problem, however good a thinker you are, will not help you, and there are two reasons why that is (that I can think of):

- You can only think of things that you know about
- You can only think of a few things at the same time

So, firstly, the Untangler technique - or anything that involves another person observing and reflecting back the unconscious elements of your thoughts - is a good way to bring to your attention elements of the problem that you did not have conscious awareness of, and therefore which you couldn't have thought about.

The collecting stage is very important in achieving this. If you ask the client specific questions, you are constraining their responses. When they talk freely, they don't know the significance of what they're saying. Whilst the story they tell you in the first stage of the technique is undoubtedly edited, it contains the structure of the 'problem', and that structure will reveal itself in multiple ways which they cannot keep track of. While the client is busy censoring what they tell you, they cannot help but reveal the truth.

Incidentally, this is one reason why coaching is so effective. One of the most important things I do is to point out or reflect back information that my clients are not consciously aware of. I am frequently called 'insightful' for doing nothing more than reflecting back something a client said ten minutes before whilst rambling on about a problem. When people talk about problems, they frequently go round in circles of logic, but the problem is so big they can't see that they are going round in circles, like a man lost in the desert who walks for miles and ends up back where he started. When I help pin the logical loop down so that they can interact with it directly, it often looks like magic. In reality, I'm simply paying attention.

A client was telling me about the problems in her business. She needed to hire a new consultant, but the workload meant she was doing a lot of work herself which took her away from running the business. She wanted to step back from the front line, but couldn't because of the workload. After listening to her go round the loop, I presented her thinking back to her:

"You can't hire a consultant because you're too busy, and you're too busy to step back because you don't have time to hire a consultant. What you need to do is create the time you need to hire someone."

She said, "You always have such good advice!", and, as you can see, it's not really advice at all. I simply untangled her thoughts.

Since our brains can only process a limited quantity of data (God obviously thought that 640k of memory was more than enough for any program[2]), a complex problem is literally too big to think about. What you need is a device to reduce the scale of the map so that you can plan your route. That is exactly what the Untangler exercise does - it gives you a way to see the whole map so that you can decide which areas you want to learn more about or change.

---

2   Bill Gates allegedly said this in 1981.

You can take the cards and arrange them somewhere that represents the past for you. You may want to arrange them at a point that represents an hour ago, or a week ago, or twenty years ago. You may want to arrange them far enough in the past that the problem is long since gone, but not so long ago that you forget to learn something useful from it.

The key is to distance yourself just far enough from the problem to be able to think about it differently. You can even move it around if you like, and find out where you like it best.

Notice any differences in the way that you arrange the cards to when you arranged them in the present. Often, people doing this find that the problem either gets packed away or gets separated into different issues - the specific problem itself and the useful information that you can extract from it.

You can use this as a group problem solving exercise too. Once you have collected all of the cards, the whole group can interact in questioning the patterns, gaining insights and rearranging the pattern into a communal solution. You'll learn a great deal from the information and patterns, and you'll learn a great deal from the group dynamics too.

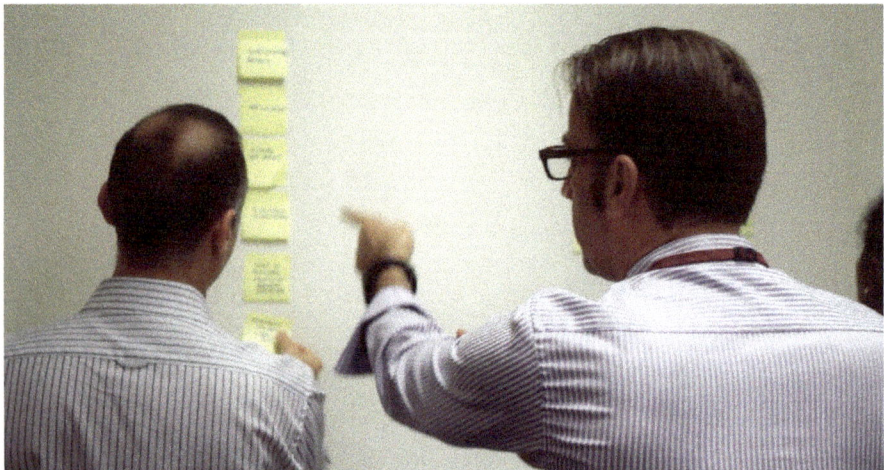

People often create problems that really reside in the future - perhaps they don't know how something will turn out, or they don't yet have enough information, or they're worrying about something. Business contingency planning is basically organised worrying, so this technique is useful here too.

The Untangler is an interesting exercise which can take many hours to complete, so make sure that you either have enough time set aside, or prepare to record the positions of the cards so that you can resume the exercise at a later time.

My advice is that the first time the client steps back and announces that they have finished organising the cards, they are far from finished. In fact, they will move fairly quickly towards a point of apparent resolution where they will then 'tinker' with the layout. Often, the client will need pushing through a fear barrier before the pattern truly resolves to its final form. You'll know it when it happens – the rush of energy from the client is sudden and tangible. What you'll be left with is a greatly simplified pattern, with cards that represent elements that are under the client's control, and the shape will have some significance for the client. The most elegant resolution for this exercise is, of course, this pattern:

Ideomotor Projection

You will need:
A human being
Optionally, some pieces of paper and a pen

mybook.li/pcip

If you have any experience as a coach then you will certainly have come across the strange phenomena whereby your client's body answers before their mouth does, or their body give you a different answer than their mouth.

The human mind and body together form a complex communication system, capable of sending and receiving multiple different messages at the same time.

Consider the fact that every input nerve in your body is attached to a primary sensory cortex in your brain, and every output nerve is connected to your motor cortex. The state of your muscles is therefore the result of whatever your brain is doing to process those sensory inputs.

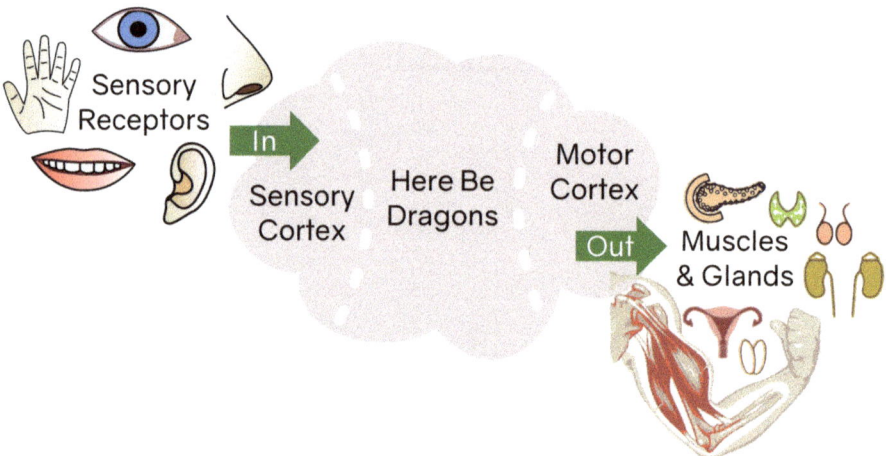

You could think of your brain, or at least the configuration of neurons in your brain, as a map of your life, containing every memory, image, sound, song lyric, unusual flavour, joyful moment… everything that you have experienced. Even if you have forgotten a particular event, it still served as the foundation for events that followed. Because of this, your experience of life has been shaped by events which took place before you even had words to describe them. From the moment you were born, the outside world was shaping every experience that you would ever have in your life.

Your brain isn't only a map of reality as it is now, it is also a map of how you would like reality to be. If you get yourself a drink while you're reading this book, that action had to be preceded by a thought, a decision, and that decision had to be preceded by a stimulus such as thirst, or a feeling that you needed to take a break, or perhaps you saw someone else with a drink.

As you decided to get a drink, your brain called upon all of your relevant past experience and organised your actions to achieve your desired result with almost no conscious planning or intervention. Your brain can organise so many parallel processes that you could easily walk, read and drink all at the same time. Be careful though, don't spill it.

Your brain is a self-correcting mechanism that is continually comparing external reality to internal desire to create motor outputs which achieve your aims and objectives and meet your various ever-changing needs.

When your desires and reality are reasonably well aligned, your motor output is simple, direct and efficient.

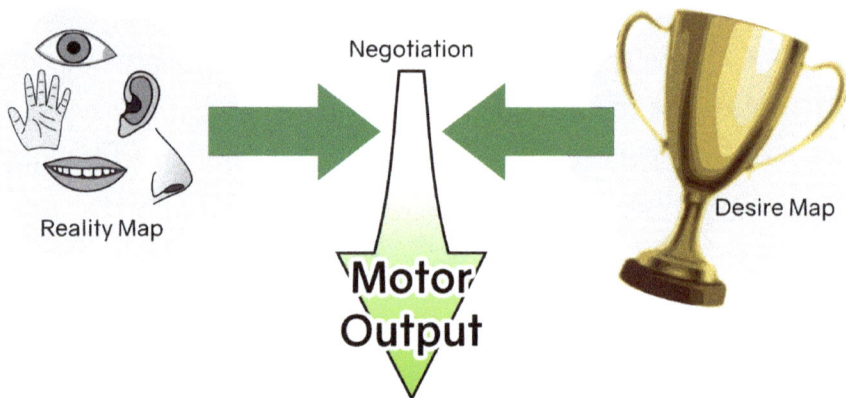

Reality Map — Negotiation — Motor Output — Desire Map

However, sometimes your desires do not adequately align with your perceived reality, and the result is internal conflict and stress. This happens when we ask any system to do too many different things at the same time. For example, if you drive a car with one foot on the accelerator pedal and one foot on the brake pedal, you can expect something to get very hot and then fall off with a 'bang'. Which is not good.

Reality Map — Negotiation — Conflict — Stress — Desire Map

When placed into a conflict configuration, the system won't be at a standstill, it will still do *something*. It just won't achieve the intended result.

That 'something' is an ideomotor response, defined by our friend Wikipedia as "a psychological phenomenon wherein a subject makes motions unconsciously". Bear in mind that 'unconsciously' does not mean 'without purpose'.

Warm or Cold

As a child, I'm sure you played the game where you had to find a hidden object with the only clues being signals of 'warmer' or 'colder' from your friend. It's a nice example of how an autonomous self-correcting system will achieve great accuracy of output using very simple components and coarse feedback. Given time and honest feedback, you would be able to locate a very small object in a very large room with ease.

The TV mentalist Derren Brown played a version of this game in a large marketplace, but instead of asking his subject to indicate 'warmer' or 'colder', he simply held their arm. By feeling the change in the tension of their muscles, he could navigate to the exact location that they had in mind. There was no psychic connection, merely an awareness that people can't have a thought without it affecting their bodies. If you disagree with that last statement then consider how you can see subtle mood changes in someone you know very well. In fact, you can probably notice their mood before they do. You're able to detect tiny changes in their muscle output because you have created a very accurate 'map' of their 'normal' state.

Stepping Stones

How can we use this in coaching?

One easy way is to set up a scenario in which we force the client to respond with their body, regardless of what they think they are communicating. Whilst this is very useful as a starting point for a conversation, it also has a tremendous sense of magic to it, giving you the ability to know things about your client which they are not aware of telling you.

Let's take an example, a sales person who is having some difficulty in their job.

To begin with, ask the client to list what they think are the steps of their sales cycle. As they do so, write each one on a piece of paper. Let's say that they give you Prospecting, Opening, Developing, Negotiating and Closing.

Arrange the sheets on the floor like stepping stones:

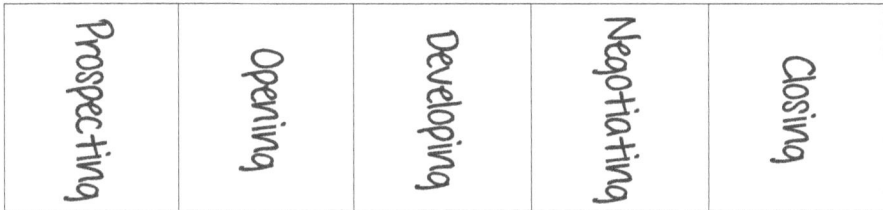

Prospecting	Opening	Developing	Negotiating	Closing

Ask your client to literally step through the sales cycle, and as they step onto each piece of paper, have them list some of the activities that they might engage in.

Having the client describe their activities engages their conscious, rational brain, and preoccupies them with what they think they are telling you, whilst their body tells you what's really happening.

As they do this, pay careful attention to how they step, in particular noticing any inconsistency in the time taken to step on or off.

You might observe:

- Hesitation before stepping onto a stage
- Lingering on a stage rather than moving on
- Talking about the next stage without moving to it
- Shifting backwards and forwards

You might also notice changes in their language, such as:

- Talking in concrete or abstract terms
- Changing modal operators, from 'am' to 'can', 'will', 'might', 'could', 'would' etc
- 'Placeholder' verbs, such as 'try to', 'get' or 'have to'
- Shifting referential index, from 'I' to 'you' or 'we'
- Hesitation, Deviation or Repetition

Notice the difference between, "Prospecting - I am checking LinkedIn, looking through existing customer lists, collecting information, using databases.", and, "Opening – erm, I would be maybe sending some messages, I could try calling, I might see who I know at their company."

Listening to the changes in language takes some practice, and in general you will find the physical differences so obvious that you don't need it. However, it's worth working on your understanding of the structure of language, because then you'll be able to use an adaptation of this technique when you can't see the client, for example when working over the phone. You'll find some guidance to decoding the client's language in my book Coaching Excellence, and in an online course, Decoding Language for Coaches, which you can find at mybook.li/decoding

Workspaces

You will need:
Your desk or usual workspace

If you're currently sitting at your desk or usual workplace, take a look around you.

If you're not currently sitting at your desk or usual workplace, read this chapter when you are.

Look at what you have in front of you. Maybe a keyboard and screen, maybe a laptop computer. You probably have an area of desk space for writing. And you probably have piles of letters, receipts, cables, pens and other paraphernalia.

Some brave readers have sent in photos of their workspaces and I have reproduced them here for you to compare with your own.

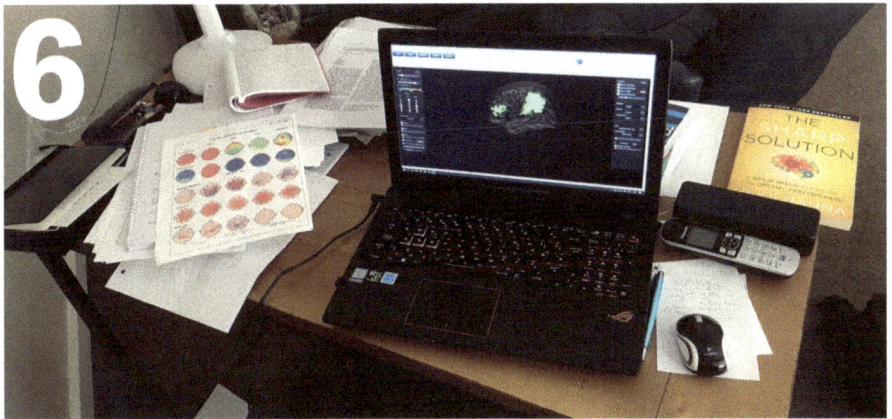

Let's imagine your workspace divided up into smaller areas:

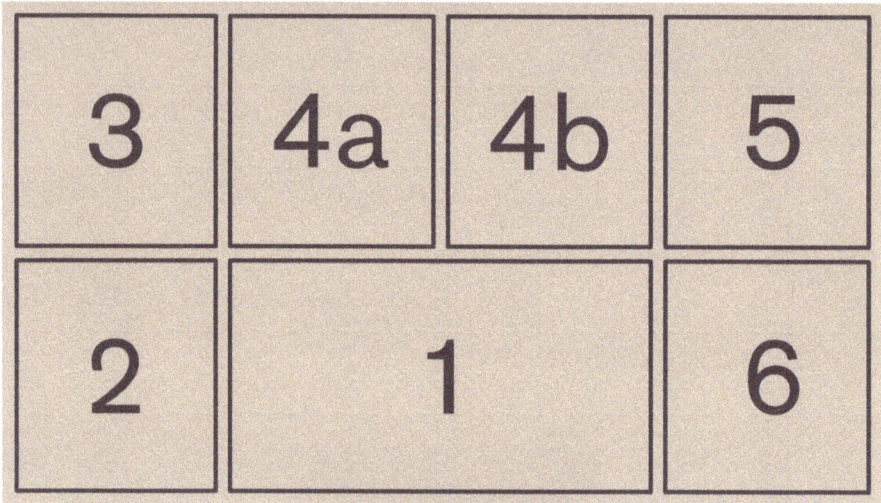

3	4a	4b	5
2	1		6

Chair

Area 4 is divided into two halves because you might find that your computer screen takes up the whole of area 4, or if not then you might find it's in a or b, or you might find that something else is going on in those areas.

As you look at your desk, what do you notice is in these areas?

Look at area 1 immediately in front of you. What does that tell you is most important to you, or you spend most of your time doing?

Look at the areas to the left and right, 2 and 3, and 5 and 6. What do those areas represent?

Do any work areas extend behind you? If so, what do you put there?

Imagine that you receive a couple of letters in the post. You need to do something with them, but not right now. They're not at all urgent. Where do you put them?

Imagine that you receive a letter that you need to deal with urgently. Where do you put it?

If you work in an office with other people, imagine someone leaves you a message on a sticky note while you're away from your desk. Where do they place it? And when you return, where do you move it to?

On my desk, I have two computer monitors, in positions 3 and 5. 4a and 4b contain slightly different things. Area 1 has my keyboard, and area 6 has my mouse, actually a trackball. If I need to write in a notebook or look through a folder, I put the keyboard on top of the things in area 4. To my left, in areas 2 and 3 are letters, meeting notes, forms waiting to be filled in, envelopes, sketches and so on. So area 2/3 appears to relate to work in progress. As I peer under the piles of paper, I discover, inexplicably, a box of Turkish delight left over from Christmas. On my right are useful tools; pens, a remote presentation control, memory cards, sticky tape, online banking code things, and inexplicably, two stickers bearing the Japanese national flag.

I suppose that I could summarise the two main storage areas as 'things I might need to do something with' and 'things I might find useful'.

I've just started doing something with the Turkish delight, and it's very nice, thank you. I haven't decided what use I have for the Japanese flags yet though.

In general, my desk is used for three types of things; things I am using now, things I might need in the near future, and things that I probably don't need but I don't know what to do with. Somewhere in the middle of the third type of things are some things that I really should deal with as a priority.

My physical workspace, and your physical workspace, is not arranged randomly. Everything that is on your desk was placed there by you, as a result of a decision about that item's role or relevance. Nothing on your desk got there by itself, unless of course there is a cat on your desk. A cat will always occupy the area that is most inconvenient to the desk owner.

Why is this useful for a coach to know about?

How a person organises their physical workspace is a reflection of how they organise their mental workspace. Regardless of what a client tells you about their working patterns, all is revealed with a simple investigation of their desk. The same decisions that dictated the placement of a letter, pen or drink will dictate the client's behaviour over the long term. A client who places important letters in a pile where they are quickly covered over might also find it difficult to take action on important decisions. The physical evidence of their procrastination is undeniable, even if the client is trying to convince you otherwise.

One student told me that he leaves 'piles' around his house. At first, he doesn't notice them, but after a time, he might walk into a room, notice the untidiness and say to himself, "Who left all this paperwork lying around?", only to then realise that it was him. On reflection, he knew that he was doing this to hide letters that made him feel like he was in trouble. It might seem paradoxical that by hiding letters, such as unpaid bills, he would actually end up in more trouble. In fact, it's not paradoxical at all, amplifying problems was precisely the purpose of the behaviour.

In the introduction to this book I mentioned the reference manual for psychiatrists, the DSM. Whereas hoarding used to be classed as an example of Obsessive Compulsive Behaviour, it is now classed as a condition in its own right; "compulsive hoarding". Now, I wouldn't class myself as a compulsive hoarder, or a hoarder of any kind, but I would say that I have things located around the house because of some future purpose that they might have. They range from batteries to screws to computer cables to paper to pens to baked beans to flour to… well, all kinds of things. There are undoubtedly things that I will never use, ever again. And there are things which I might need tomorrow. The problem is that I can't tell which is which.

If I'm a hoarder then I am also a hoarder of information and skills. I know things about a broad range of subjects. I've done lots of different jobs, and in any area of my career I have always earned a reputation as someone who will have a go at anything. Is there are correlation between this and the contents of my garden shed? I think so. Both are aspects of my need for utility.

As you look around your own workspace, or even your home, what correlations do you see between your mental and physical workspaces?

If you have the opportunity to observe the workspaces of your clients, you could gain some valuable insights into their inner workspaces which will inform and support your coaching conversations. You might even use your observations to make predictions about your clients' future behaviour, and that might even give the impression that you are psychic, prescient or simply brilliant, if you like that sort of thing.

Three Words

To finish with, a fun party trick. Or a very revealing test to discover a person's true nature.

First, think of your favourite colour. Write down three different words (or short phrases) that describe what your favourite colour is like - what it means to you.

Second, if you could have any animal - real or imaginary - as a pet, what would it be? Write down three different words (or short phrases) that describe the qualities of your pet.

Third, imagine yourself swimming in the ocean. You have dived beyond your depth and you realise that you don't have enough air in your lungs to reach the surface. You then find that you can breathe underwater. Write down three different words (or short phrases) that describe this experience.

Finally, imagine yourself standing in a room where everything around you is completely white. Write down three different words (or short phrases) that describe this experience.

Once the three words in four categories have been written down by you, or your friend, client or potential love interest, you can reveal the hidden meaning.

The words you used to describe your favourite colour reveal how you see yourself.

The words you used to describe your ideal pet reveal how your friends see you.

The words you used to describe your experience of breathing underwater are how you describe your experience of sex.

The words you used to describe the white room reveal how you think of or feel about death.

You can also find an online version of this at mybook.li/pctw

Full Circle

Well, here we are again. Right back where we started. We've walked a path together, and it has led us on an adventure, but unless we bring what we have learned back into our everyday lives, our adventure is lost, forgotten.

In 1949, Joseph Campbell wrote 'The Hero with a Thousand Faces', an analysis of the structure of mythology which followed the archetype of the hero on a journey of self-discovery. This structure, which Campbell termed the 'monomyth', could be seen in stories told in every language, and in literature stretching back thousands of years. Clearly, the hero's journey has not been constrained by differences in national languages. From Star Wars to Finding Nemo, from Homer's Odyssey to Marvel's Iron Man, the story of the hero reflects our own journey through life. We set out on new adventures, meet guides and mentors, cross great chasms, vanquish our dragons and arrive home, victorious.

If you're old enough, or young enough, to have read the books of Julia Donaldson then you might have enjoyed 'A Squash and a Squeeze' in which a little old lady who lives in a tiny, cramped, overcrowded house takes all her pets on a long journey to the other side of the purple mountains in order to find somewhere new to live. Her pets know that they are in fact walking in a circle, as they begin to appreciate the beautiful views and the many joys of the countryside. As they arrive back at their starting point, the old lady finds an empty cottage which perfectly meets her needs. It is no longer tiny and cramped, now it is cosy and snug, the perfect size for her and her pets.

Perhaps you too have had the experience that you only fully appreciate what you have today when you have experienced a much greater frame of reference to compare yourself to.

Maybe that experience has been as ordinary as returning from a holiday and seeing your home in a new light. Maybe that experience has been dramatic and life changing. In either case, what that experience brought you was a new perspective, a new context within which to make a new meaning for the familiar aspects of your life.

As coaches, we are transforming lives, and that journey must begin with our own. This isn't so that we can stand on a stage and grin at the audience with our shiny white dental veneers, like a lighthouse of hope beaming out to the needy. This is so that we can understand and empathise with the journey of self-discovery, and through our own journey, recognise that we are separate and distinct from our clients. We can understand them, but we are not them. I see so many coaches leap into a conversation with, "That happened to me! I know exactly how you feel!". No. You don't. You know how you felt. That was a valuable experience, but it belonged to you, no-one else. Your temptation to project yourself into the mind of your clients can now be replaced with a carefully selected kit of projective coaching techniques. You have no need to be 'in there' with your clients when you can so easily enable them to bring their experiences 'out here' in a way which transcends the limitations of language and the constraints of 'powerful coaching questions'.

With a new freedom to express the myriad of life's rich experience, we transform and transcend that experience; for ourselves, for our clients, for all of the lives that we touch.

Acknowledgements

I would like to thank, in no particular order, the following people who were each very important in bringing this book into reality. Thank you so much for your kind contributions, your sharing, your inspiration and your fellowship on this peculiar journey that we call life.

Emma Freeth

Millie Freeth

Isobel Freeth

Adrian Hales

Jess Wall

Stuart Betteridge

Jamie Beaumont

Anthony Taylor

Abi Edmunds

David Willmore

Nicholas Paton Philip

Mariana González García

Corin Gasdoiu

Roy Lane

Jeanette Cowley

David Wise

Francois Coetzee

John Lesley

Henrietta Laitt

Tatiana Stewart

David Morgan

Eleanor Hayes

Poonam Tewari Jalan

Rym Abdelkhalek Rachdi

Amanda Menahem

Christine Chapman

Matthew Doyle

Albert Chong

Stormie Sandhu

Giuliano Papadia

Kathryn Fisher

Helen McDermott

Gary Link

Charles Lambdin

Patrick Armstrong

Devi Cattell